THE POWER OF

MIRACLE

THINKING

"The Power of Miracle Thinking
is pure inspiration and a
genuine resource of hope!"
– Caroline Myss

RANDY PEYSER

The Power of Miracle Thinking
© 2008 Randy Peyser. All Rights Reserved.

Published in the USA by:
Author One Stop
www.AuthorOneStop.com

ISBN 978-0-9796629-1-1 0-9796629-1-5

Printed in the United States of America.

Book design by Darlene Swanson of Van-garde Imagery, Inc.
Cover design by Renne Rhae of RRhae Art Studios

The Power of Miracle Thinking

"*The Power of Miracle Thinking* is pure inspiration and a genuine resource of hope!" – Caroline Myss, Author of *Entering the Castle*

"*The Power of Miracle Thinking* is wonderful, inspiring, and highly empowering. From the first page to the last it is uplifting and will give the reader the faith they need to have the miracle they have been praying for!" – Dr. Terry Cole-Whittaker, Author of *What You Think of Me is None of My Business*

"Through a collection of inspiring stories and powerful tips, this book sets you firmly on the path of creating miracles in your life!" – Marci Shimoff, Author of *Happy for No Reason*, featured in *The Secret*

"Wow! Wow! Wow! Every once in a while, there is a book whose very first page to the last grabs your attention and won't let go.

The stories are unforgettable, and yet, I am compelled to go back and read them again and again." – Gloria Wendroff, Author of *Heavenletters*

"Randy Peyser moves you swiftly from a spectator of other people's miracles into the future of your life. . . . so you, too, can participate fully in creating your own miracles. I love this book!" – Mary Ellen "Angelscribe," Author of *Expect Miracles*

"*The Power of Miracle Thinking* is filled with inspiring stories of "real" people we can identify with. While some books recount stories of miracles, Randy Peyser has taken this a step further by clearly explaining the mindsets and actions of those who create miracles. In so doing, Randy has given us the tools to create our own miracles." – Jeff Keller, Author of *Attitude is Everything*

Dedication

This book is lovingly dedicated to the memory of
Reverend Delorise 'Momma' Lucas, who once said,
"Randy, don't let nobody steal your joy!"

Acknowledgments

I wish to acknowledge and thank those people who have been my teachers and mentors, and who have helped me to continually refine my Miracle Thinking mindset: the late Reverend Delorise Lucas, who only saw the good in people; Harriet Peyser, my mother, who insists that 'attitude is everything'; Suzanne Baker, my partner, who creates at least one miracle every day; Gary Douglas, an extraordinary facilitator of consciousness; Krystyna Barron, who helps me move mountains in minutes; Jill Lublin, who taught me how to 'walk on sunshine'; Sandra Bond, my agent; and Darius Gottlieb, who understands the inner workings of an Eepster.

A giant 'thank you' goes to all of the wonderful contributors whose stories and insights grace these pages. You have taught me by example, and I am honored and grateful that you have chosen to share your experiences to help light the way for all.

Thank you to: Suzanne Baker, Dawna Markova, MaryEllen Angelscribe, Debra LeForest, Cari Alter, Katherine Revoir,

Peggy Black, Christine Hodil, Lila Harding, Robert Plath, Sandy Alemian, Norm Mosher, Barb Rees, Nadia McCaffrey, Rayna Lumbard, Elissa Giles, Kathleen Ronald, Krystyna Barron, Thomas Day Oates, Steven Walters, Ronnie Chittum, Dallas Franklin, Mike Fink, Susan Gilbert, Linda Peterson, Joe Westerhaver, Terri Amos, Helena Hennessey, Una Versailles, Adano Henderson, Betty Anne Sayers, J.J. Crow, Nancy L. Herhahn, Karen Williams, Kathleen Casey, Elyse Killoran, David Franklin, Ellen Henson, and Suzka!

Table of Contents

Introduction

- Steven Walters was given 24 hours to live. Ten years later, he still shows no signs of leukemia.

- A fire, which consumed 500,000 acres, swept across Ronnie Chittum's property in Southern Oregon. While everything in every direction burnt to the ground, Ronnie's home remained untouched.

- Professional speaker, Kathleen Ronald, makes no sales calls to attract new clients, yet ever since she began her business, her phone has been ringing off the hook, and she speaks before thousands of people every year.

Each of these people has quite a different story, yet they all had one thing in common – each experienced something that can't easily be explained away. Some might call what they each experienced 'a miracle.'

In the course of writing this book, I wanted to know if it was possible to influence the possibility of a miracle occurring. For example, could we create miraculous results on a consistent basis by changing our thoughts, beliefs and attitudes, or by performing certain actions? Or were miracles simply doled out at random by some unseen force over which we have no influence? After interviewing many people who have experienced miracles, on the following pages, you will learn what I discovered.

Meet the Miracle Thinkers

Did you ever notice how sometimes we work hard and struggle, while other times, things seem to flow more easily to us? Often, when we desire more money, success, a relationship, greater abundance, or good health, we take the necessary action steps, say a few prayers for good measure, then wait for our miracle to unfold. However, when our desired outcome doesn't readily appear, we invariably lose hope. In fact, at some point we might feel so frustrated or stuck that we begin to wonder if we're going to spend the rest of our lives making nests out of pencil shavings.

Why is it that while everyone goes through tough times, clearly some people seem to weather these storms with greater ease? Why is it that some people achieve great success or prevail, in spite of the overwhelming difficulties that surface in their lives? Obviously, people like Steven, Ronnie and Kathleen did something that enabled them to open a door, as if by magic, to move them toward their goals. I call people like Steven, Ronnie and Kathleen, "Miracle Thinkers."

What Constitutes a Miracle?

For official purposes, let's call a miracle an unexpected manifestation, or the creation of any uplifting desire that appears to be provided through what could only be called Grace. A miracle can be an unforeseen act, a prayed for act, or the creation of anything wonderful in your life that you really want but are not sure is truly possible. Unofficially, let's call a miracle any occurrence that makes you say, "Wow! That was a miracle!"

What is Miracle Thinking?

Miracle Thinking is about developing the kind of mindset that leads to the growing of miracles in one's life. *The Power of Miracle Thinking* is a guidebook for people who want to consistently produce miracles. I'm not talking about walking on water; I'm talking about creating something you've always wanted, like an increase in money, finding your soul mate, healing a physical ailment, overcoming an obstacle, achieving greater joy, and the "biggee" for many people – creating one's dream. This collection includes the true stories of many people who have used Miracle Thinking strategies to create the results they wanted. At the end of every story are Miracle Thinking Tips that you can put to use in your life right now.

What Miracle Thinking Is Not

While miracles are given through Grace, Miracle Thinkers have learned that they can contribute to the creation of their desired results through the power of the thoughts they hold, and the attitudes or feeling states they maintain. However, "Miracle Thinking" is not just about having a positive attitude. You can't tell anyone, "Just change your attitude, be happy, and things will work out," and expect them to change. We change by unwrapping the layers one-by-one that are not Miracle Thinking. Sometimes those layers take days and sometimes they take years. It is also not our responsibility to judge another or demand that anyone else change. Instead, Miracle Thinkers choose to focus on developing their own personal abilities.

You Don't Have To Be a Superhero

Here is another thing you will want to know about Miracle Thinkers – being a Miracle Thinker does not necessarily mean you have to have it together all the time. Sometimes we react, overreact, slump, despair, panic or feel stuck. We get depressed, we feel fragile, we lose it, or we feel lost. However, being a Miracle Thinker means that, sooner or later, we will pick ourselves up and dust ourselves off. We will remember. We will make new choices. We will choose peace. We will endure, get through it, strengthen, grow, and learn.

More often than not, Miracle Thinkers:

- Make choices and take actions that continually lead to the cultivation of a miracle mindset.

- Express themselves without censoring themselves out of the fear of being judged.

- Step into and live their truth.

- Choose to never withhold anything from anyone for any length of time.

- Take action that supports their growth.

- Make phone calls and do follow-ups.

- Let go of the victim stance.

- Step away from that which is not for their Highest Good.

- Say 'yes' to life more often than they say 'no.'

- Move with the flow.

Same God, Different Wrapper

In truth, everyone has a piece of the Miracle Thinking puzzle because each of us has a unique point of reference. It is the purpose of this book to invite a larger dialogue in which anyone who so desires can contribute to the Miracle Thinking conversation.

What I've discovered is that Miracle Thinkers come from all spiritual traditions, religions, and walks of life. No particular group, person, religion, tradition, or philosophy owns the market when it comes to miracles, and no one particular group, religion or tradition is represented in this book. Throughout this book, if the word, "God," is not your reference point, please use a word that holds greater meaning for you.

What's Ahead?

In the following stories, you'll read about people who have created incomes beyond their wildest dreams; who have turned around life-threatening conditions or defied death; who have overcome hair-raising obstacles; or who have found their soul mates, and much more. While their stories and circumstances are very different, the one thing they all have in common is that each used Miracle Thinking concepts to create their desired outcome.

A Caveat

As you develop your ability as a Miracle Thinker, you might notice results beginning to occur immediately. On the other hand, if you feel like you are wading through molasses and that it's taking forever to create your desired outcome, one of four things is possible: 1) either you are not clearly aligned with your perceived goal and a part of you still fears the achievement of it; 2) the goal you've chosen is not for your Highest Good; 3) the timing just isn't right; 4) or you might be going through what I call, "W-A-I-T Training," in which case there are more things for you to learn before you can have what it is you want.

The Big Trump Card

In the following stories, you will learn powerful Miracle Thinking strategies to help you overcome fear and other forms of internal resistance that might be keeping you at arm's length from your desired goals and miracles. However, if your desired outcome involves a timing issue, there are usually people you need to meet or resources you need to have, which aren't in place yet. Divine Right Timing always trumps our own sense of what we think the timing of circumstances in our lives should be. You also cannot manipulate the Universe into giving anything to you. When no doors seem to be opening, think of this time as the 'Ripening Time.' Even if you are already a very deep person, it is guaranteed that you are being deepened even more by the Divine Source that created you.

About Faith

Miracle Thinking is strengthened by faith. If your faith is strong, does this mean that your desired miracle will happen every time? It won't if the result you've chosen is not in your highest and best interest. However, cultivating a Miracle Thinking mindset will move you closer to receiving the Highest Good that is intended for you, which may or may not bring you the specific outcome you desire. The trick is to maintain your Miracle Thinking mindset and keep staying the course, regardless.

Ask Yourself This Question . . .

When circumstances in my life felt overwhelming and I could not see my way out, I would ask myself, "How would a Miracle Thinker hold this experience?" Asking this question always helped me to refocus my perception in a new way. When you are in a tough spot, ask yourself this question: "How would a Miracle Thinker hold this experience?" Allow the answer to come to you in any way that it makes itself known to you.

By asking yourself this question, as well as by reading the following stories and tips, it is my sincere desire that you are inspired to develop your own Miracle Thinking mindset so that you, too, can consistently achieve miracles in your life.

Special Notes

To find out more about the Miracle Thinkers who have contributed their stories, many have provided a brief bio and their contact information in the back of the book.

***BONUS:** You can download a beautifully designed, free mini-poster of some of the top Miracle Thinking strategies. This page is available to my readers as a 'thank you' for having purchased this book. **For your free mini-poster, please go to: www.miraclethinking.com/readerspecial.htm**.*

*If you would like to share your thoughts and experiences about miracles, or to read more Miracle Thinking stories, please visit: **www.miraclethinking.com**.*

Here's to the abundant creation of all your heart's desires!

Randy Peyser

"A 'no' just means you are not talking to the right person. If someone tells you 'no,' keep on going until you find the person who says, 'yes.'"

– Krystyna Barron

For Making Your Dreams Come True . . .

The Sting

In 1988, Krystyna Barron lost her job in a corporate merger right after her boyfriend, Craig, had taken a leave of absence from his job as a cameraman. Looking at their dwindling financial situation, the pair mulled over the idea of starting an effects company for the movie industry in which they would create matte paintings. These were very realistic paintings done on glass that would be combined with live-action, motion-picture photography to create backgrounds.

With his experience in film, Craig would handle the photography and Krystyna would run the business, while another friend would handle the artwork. However, after the trio did a tiny job for HBO, none of them felt motivated to continue, so they packed up their stuff and forgot about it.

When neither Krystyna nor Craig had secured a job in nine month's time, they decided to revisit their idea. Once again, they contacted HBO, and this time, a very large job was on the table.

The discussion was going quite well until the corporate executive requested a visit to their facility. Obviously, he wanted to make sure the newly-formed company could deliver the results he needed. He would arrive on their doorstep in one week!

At this point, their fledgling company, "Matte World," was nothing more than a name, with a credit list of a few small jobs and a staff of two, since the artist had returned to Oregon. They had no studio, no employees, and no equipment – other than 2 cameras, a tripod, an artist's easel, a drafting table and some odds and ends.

With not a second to spare, they decided to set up a mock facility. First, they leased an empty warehouse space for one month – which, according to Krystyna, was a miracle in itself since industrial landlords usually do not agree to such short lease terms. Then they rented office furniture, portable dividing walls and tons of plants. They also rented cameras and lights, created sets, and hung matte paintings and other effects stuff on the walls. Artists' easels exhibiting works in progress and camera stations were set up, while rows of empty file cabinets lined the fake office walls.

Since there were no electrical outlets, they glued electrical boxes with 4 outlets to the walls and plugged in bunches of cords. "Although everything was a prop, it all had to look real. It was Matte World's version of "The Sting," says Krystyna.

Once the props were in place, they called every friend they could think of who might be available to come over and pretend to be an "employee" the day of the HBO exec's visit. Of course, they also brought in all kinds of equipment, miniatures and artwork so their friends would all be able to pretend they were working, painting, drawing, doing camera tests, etc.

Then they ran into one major problem – the phone. This was at a time before cell phones, and no doubt, the HBO executive would ask to use the phone. Creating more miracles, Krystyna got the phone company to install a working line in one day's time. Next, they arranged for other friends to call in every five minutes to create the illusion that the business was "happening."

When the HBO executive arrived, the couple entertained him with a delightful lunch at a restaurant next door to their "studio," making sure to use the restrooms at the restaurant, since there wasn't one in their warehouse space. Then they enticed and distracted their guest with a slide show. Since there was no electricity in their warehouse, and they needed electricity for the slide projector, they had made a deal with an adjacent tenant, who was a mountain bike manufacturer, to fish an extension cord over the adjoining wall to their space and use his electrical outlet.

The executive was delighted with Matte World and awarded them the job during his visit. As he left, the gang dropped everything and started to applaud. Just then the executive came back in to hand the pair a deposit check – and use the phone. Everyone was stunned for a moment, but quickly resumed their acts.

The result? The effects they created for that particular project won Matte World the Emmy for Best Visual Effects! Since then, Matte World Digital has worked on over 100 major feature films. They are used by all of the big studios and directors, and have garnered an Oscar nomination in England and the United States.

Miracle Thinking Tips

❋ When an opportunity comes knocking at your door, will you sabotage yourself by saying that you are not ready, or will you find a way to make it happen? Miracle Thinkers believe in themselves and "act as if." They proceed forward as if their desired outcome must come about. Craig knew they had the ability that the HBO exec needed. What they didn't have was the facility – the façade, the outer trappings – that would convince the exec that they could handle the job. In what might be considered an extraordinary act of chutzpah, Krystyna and Craig immediately jumped into gear to make their dreams come true. They chose to "act as if," and by doing so, they literally opened the (fake studio) door for miracles to happen.

❋ Did you ever have an idea and tell it to someone only to have him or her give you all the reasons that it couldn't happen? Did you buy into their reasoning (like somehow they knew better than you) and let it stop you from creating your idea? Did the idea dissolve away? Did you try every possibility? Says Krystyna, "I function from the framework that "almost anything is possible" and move forward on as many possibilities as I can think of. When I am told 'no,' I do not automatically accept it and shut down. 'No' is a response that propels me to search for the 'yes,' or to find a different person to ask. You'd be amazed at the variety of responses you can get if you ask to speak to someone different."

As you visualize the future possibility of a creation, pay attention to any obstacles that pop up in your mind. In addition to "acting as if," Krystyna imagined the potential "what ifs." 'What if' the HBO exec. asked to use a bathroom? 'What if' he needed to use the phone? 'What if' he had too much time to take a close look at the façade? As a result of visualizing the potential "what ifs," the pair created a plan that included a long lasting lunch where they were able to conduct the majority of their business, arranged for a working phone, and strategically placed a comment about using the restrooms while at the restaurant, which easily persuaded the Exec to use the bathroom without discovering that they didn't have one!

*"I realized that 'my type'
was screwed up, so I started
praying for somebody who
wasn't 'my type'."*

– Cari Alter

For Finding "The One" . . .

The One

In the fourteenth year of her marriage, Cari Alter felt that the chasm between herself and her husband was as wide as the Grand Canyon. Without realizing it, they had an unspoken agreement that they would always operate as if everything was okay no matter what. In the process, Cari found herself compromising her own needs for the sake of being the perfect wife and mother. Although at first, it seemed as though her husband was responsible for the problems in their relationship, it slowly became clear to her that putting her own needs on the shelf was the real source of her angst.

The message hit home loud and clear the day she went to a doctor's appointment and discovered there was a strong possibility that she might have cancer. In response to the rather dire news, she actually found herself feeling happy. At that moment, she realized something was very wrong. Why was she feeling happy about the possibility of dying? She realized that if she died, she would never have to go through all the pain that comes with a divorce. In that moment, she realized how deeply unhappy she really was in the marriage, regardless of the fact that she still loved her husband.

Cari felt like a grenade had exploded inside of her; neither staying or going felt like an option. Additionally, she believed that leaving the marriage would only result in her repeating the same dysfunctional patterns with somebody else. She made a vow to stay in the relationship until she "could see God" in her husband; she would stay in her marriage until she could feel love for him for who he was in his true essence, and until she no longer felt the need to make him wrong.

As the years passed, the day finally came when she knew she had to get divorced. However, the pain of that realization was so excruciating that, on that particular evening, she felt as though she wanted to literally climb out of her own skin. In desperation, not knowing what to do, she grabbed a book that had the picture of a spiritual master on its cover, and held it to her chest. The first time Cari had ever noticed this book, she had visibly seen a beam of light shoot directly into her heart from the face on that cover. Holding the book now, she began to feel a sense of relief and gradually fell asleep. Upon awakening and still clutching the book to her chest, she discovered that her pain had greatly diminished.

By gazing for long periods into the eyes of the image of the master, Cari began to develop a deep feeling of connection with her Divine Self, that part of oneself that merges with God. This developing connection with the Divine brought her a greater sense of trust in life itself. "Trust comes from feeling connected.

If I'm not trusting the depth of my connection, I need to turn inward and strengthen my connection to Source," she says. Within time, as she strengthened within, the warm, full glow of her spiritual connection replaced the need to make her husband wrong.

Three months later, the couple separated. With the old pattern of suppressing anger gone, fighting now erupted in a way that it never had during their marriage. When the child support payments were not forthcoming, Cari found herself feeling quite justified in making her former spouse wrong again.

Finally, she made a decision to stop fighting; no matter what happened, she decided that she would hold "a vision of him being happy and successful in his own life." Very quickly, she noticed that "everything shifted and he started making the payments on time."

For the following year, Cari felt no desire to date anybody. Then, quite by surprise, she met a man at a party who was 'her type.' Within three weeks, however, she realized that this was the exact same type of relationship she'd just left. "I realized that 'my type' was screwed up," says Cari, "so I started praying for somebody who wasn't 'my type.'" A series of men paraded ever so briefly into her life, each encounter ending almost as quickly as it had begun.

One day, Cari decided to consult a spiritual healer and psychic, and was told, "Your man is coming, a tall man. You are going to meet him by the end of July, and this is going to be 'the one.'" Trusting the purveyor of the message, Cari decided to make a list of the attributes that she would like to have in a partner. While most individuals might list 10 or so attributes, Cari listed 90!

On July 28, she was introduced by phone to a man named

David, who was a friend of a friend. When the two talked, Cari suggested that they meet for a picnic and a hike, since hiking was definitely on Cari's list. As it turned out, this tall man was an avid hiker. Cooking was another big consideration on her list. Would David's idea of a picnic be to show up with just some cheese and bread? Cari was not to be disappointed. When David revealed his offering, it turned out to be chicken in a homemade, coconut-curry sauce; he was a gourmet cook.

"Out of 90 things on my list, he had 80 of the attributes I listed," says Cari. "After the first month or two, he picked up another 8. He was only 2 short," she says with a laugh.

Did Cari instantly know that he was 'the one?'

"I had no feeling of knowing that he was the one," she says. "When he first opened the door and I looked at him, I thought, 'Oh well, he'll definitely make a good friend.' I wasn't physically attracted to him because I'd asked for someone who wasn't my type." In the process of taking many hikes and spending much quality time together, however, the pair drew closer, and Cari's 'type' began to change.

"I probably wouldn't have allowed him to get that close if I'd been considering him relationship material," says Cari. "I had always been with men who were not emotionally available and who wouldn't spend much time with me. Here was a man who was spending time with me and who was being emotionally intimate. I'd also never dated a younger man. David was eleven years younger than me, but he was the first grownup I'd ever dated. He's the only one who was emotionally mature."

Cari had finally found "Mr. Right," and the couple has been together ever since.

Miracle Thinking Tips

* Are you torn about staying in a relationship or ending it? "The time to leave is when there is no more reason to leave," says Cari. "As long as I had reason to leave, I was making my husband wrong, which meant that I was still tied to him. If I tried to leave him, I would only have recreated the same type of relationship because I was still connected to whatever I was making him wrong about. When you can finally see the God in another person, and you aren't making that person wrong anymore, then there is no reason to leave, and there is no reason to stay. At that point, you can freely choose to leave. If, however, you are leaving because of a reason, then you are not leaving from a place of free choice. You are leaving because things are terrible, or because things are whatever way your personality evaluates them to be. Once you have no reason to leave, then you can leave from free choice and choose a different life."

* If you want to attract miracles into your life, Cari suggests the following: "Imagine that you have a nickel for every thought that you have or word that you say. Divide your nickels into two piles; one pile represents every good thought you have, every kindness you've expressed, and every action that feels good to you; the other represents every negative thought, judgment or worry. At the end of your life which pile do you think is going to be higher?

Every moment, you can make a choice as to which pile you are going to add a nickel to. A miracle is something that would go in the positive pile. So if your thoughts are going toward positive things, you will attract more miracles."

* "The more time that you spend with either pile, the more the nickels will just naturally flow toward that pile. The negative pile is exclusive of miracles. In that mindset, miracles will not happen. Negative thoughts are like fly paper; they're sticky. Just like a fly, a negative thought will fly by and the next thing you know, you're stuck. Fortunately, positive thoughts can be sticky, too. Therefore, the more positive thoughts you have, the more positive thoughts you will generate, and the more miracles you will receive. What you now call miracles will then become just a way of life."

Keep following the 'Divine Threads.' Your 'Divine Threads' will lead you to identify what it is you are here to do."

– Katherine Revoir

Holy Cow!

With her marriage on the rocks, fine artist, Katherine Revoir, decided that portrait painting would be the quickest way to make money to support herself and her two children. However, upon launching her new career, the artist soon found commercial portrait painting to be like "fingernails on the blackboard of her soul."

To break up the drudgery of portraiture, she decided to do something just for fun. So she got out her jigsaw and cut out a cow from some plywood, painted it to look real, and stuck it in her backyard. Everybody commented on how fabulous the cow was. People even started asking if they could buy one. One day, through a connection from a friend, Katherine showed her cow to a Gift Rep in San Francisco. She immediately said, "I can sell these."

Within a week, Katherine had orders for 150 cows – with no idea how to mass-produce them. Her original one had been cut out and hand-painted. Out of necessity, she hurriedly figured out how to have her cows screen-printed and mass-produced.

Within six months, her cows were featured in catalogues all over the country. She expanded her efforts and began screen-printing her cows on t-shirts. "This was 1988, a time when cows were all the rage. If there was a cow on it, it would sell," says Katherine.

When the boxes of t-shirts and stacks of cows overtook every bit of her living room and garage, she moved the business into a warehouse. Within four years, she had expanded into three large warehouses, and her gross sales were $2.5 million from t-shirts and other manufactured products with her artwork on them.

Then her life took an unexpected turn. "Every corner of my life was in crisis at the same time," says Katherine. "My mother was diagnosed with lung cancer. My eleven-year-old son was in trouble at school. The love of my life dumped me unceremoniously, and the market changed in the gift industry away from t-shirts, and towards candles, picture frames, and other household products."

Katherine finally started listening to the small, inner voice that had been nudging her for two years to make a change. But by this time, the small voice had escalated to an annoying roar. She knew only two things: 1) she had to close the business, or the business would close in on her, and 2) something was spiritually calling her, and it would not reveal itself until she cleared away the dramatic debris of her life.

By the time she closed the business and the loans were paid off, Katherine was left with fifteen cents in her bank account. Unclear about her direction, the only thing she knew for certain was that she wanted to combine her creativity in some way with her spirituality. "I knew that, spiritually, it was possible for me to do whatever

I wanted, but I had to get clear on the 'what.' After that, I needed to have absolute faith and conviction in the ability of my God Self to show up with everything I needed to make this happen."

Katherine was led to her next step when her ten-year-old niece asked her for a birthday present that wasn't "boring." Searching through a bookstore, she couldn't find anything that a ten-year-old might think was cool. So she decided to create a book herself. The book featured a series of scenarios in which her niece was asked to do things like create a TV show and give it a name, describe the characters, and design and draw the costumes.

Katherine had so much fun putting the book together that she decided to send a copy of it to a publisher. Six months later, she landed her first book deal for her journal and sketchbook that encouraged expressive writing, drawing and thinking for young adults. However, to Katherine's dismay, the editor deleted the spiritual scenarios, such as: "If you were going to talk with God, what would you say?"

One day, she heard her inner voice proclaiming, "You will do a book for adults, which is *just* about spiritual stuff." Katherine didn't consider herself a writer, but her inner voice said, "All you have to do is show up at your drawing table every day, and we'll take care of the rest." By this time, Katherine was in a "best friend" relationship with her inner guidance, so she listened and took action. Fourteen months later, her second book was released, which helps one access inner guidance and expand creative self-expression. Currently, Katherine is a ministerial student, continuing on her journey of combining spirituality and creative self-expression.

Miracle Thinking Tips

✦ Searching for your purpose? Says Katherine, "When I was nine years old, I heard a voice tell me that I was here to do something very important. What I realized after all these years is that we are all here to do something important. We are all here for very specific purposes. How do you identify your purpose if you haven't got a clue? Just follow and keep following the 'Divine Threads,' which are those things that you love, exciting opportunities, or things that scare you a little bit or make your hands feel clammy. Your Divine threads will lead you to identify what it is you are here to do."

✦ "When you plant a carrot seed, don't expect to get a sunflower," says Katherine. "We live in a world of cause and effect. That's how the universe works. The creative process of the universe involves planting a seed and nourishing it. If you take those steps, it must grow. It's the law. So if you have a desire to be a writer, for example, and you're willing to nourish your seed with spiritual practice, supportive people, and keeping your own mind out of the gutter in terms of any limiting beliefs, thoughts, and attitudes, then your seed will grow. It has to."

✦ "Developing a relationship with your Higher Power will help you navigate the rough spots of your life path. Rather than thinking that you are out there all alone, struggling to actualize a dream or just trying to get through the day, you can lean on the Universal Life Force that not only created you, but while It was at it, sent you into this life with a road map and plans for expressing your soul's work as only you can do. If you were raised in a religion that does not feed your soul spiritually, find one that does."

"Dream BIG for you can't stuff a great life into a small dream."

– Barb Rees

The Geriatric Gypsies

Barb Rees and her husband, Dave, a.k.a., the "Geriatric Gypsies," were riding high on the heady updraft of the aroma of freedom. They'd just flown the coup of their day-to-day lives with only $300 in their pockets. For a long time, they'd dreamt of traveling across Canada, but while their pensions would cover their home expenses while they were gone, $300 would hardly be enough to drive across their entire country in an old, gas-guzzling motor home. However, the two believed that if a dream had been given to them by the universe, then the universe also knew that they had the power to make that dream come true, *if* only they had the faith.

Prior to their grand adventure, the couple decided to sell products at farmer's markets as they traveled in order to pay their way across the country. Dave created works of art out of driftwood, while Barb canned 102 jars of brandied blackberry sauce to sell. The two also placed signs around their house, which read, "Choose faith over fear, for a little faith can move mountains."

Whenever doubts seeped in, they'd read their sign out loud. Upon awakening, the first thing they saw every morning was a large Canadian map, which displayed their carefully marked route.

Before they left, support began to flood in. The blackberries were all donated, at times from absolute strangers. People prayed for them and encouraged them. Barb and Dave would look at one another and think, "How can we not be successful with all this positive energy and love?"

Barb had also written a book called, "Lessons from the Potholes of Life," which she could sell along the way. The premise of her book was that one could dig diamonds out difficulties. Now was certainly the time to put her premise to the test.

In late June, they left the west coast of British Columbia, looking like Ma and Pa Kettle, as they hit the road in their jam-packed, 27-foot motor home, which had driftwood piled high on the roof, canned goods and Barb's books in every nook, and a big box attached to the back that contained a huge root system.

The following morning, they displayed their wares at the first of 34 markets in which they would participate across 9 provinces. The love and support of the vendors and the general public filled them with enthusiasm.

Slowly, they climbed pass after pass through the rugged territory of British Columbia, then headed for Barb's family reunion in Calgary. Calgary came to be the oasis in their trip, both coming and going. There, they could relax and enjoy the hospitality and love of family. "Every dreamer has to have an oasis to run to for refreshment," says Barb.

On their journey, many times they were given food and supplies from total strangers. They called these regular outpourings of love, "Gifts of Abundance." Each morning they would ask the universe, "What gifts of abundance will you send us today?" Even if it meant that they had paid for 10 onions and received 15, they always knew they were receiving gifts of abundance from the universe and gave thanks.

Each farmer's market brought new friends, new ideas, new lessons and enough income to get them to the next event. However, there were many moments when it looked like there wouldn't be enough money to proceed. Yet, somehow they did. Only twice in all of the 34 markets and in 25 different towns, did they not make back their booth fee. No matter how low they felt, the next market would always dispel their fears.

In Thunder Bay, Barb sold the last of the 102 jars of her sauce. They made great friends among the vendors, and received more produce and support. It was becoming evident by this point that the principle of not waiting for the lights to all be green at the same time before you follow your dream was at play in their lives.

At their next farmer's market, they endured an all-day thunderstorm, yet were blessed with excellent sales in driftwood. Says Barb, "When dreamers are motivated by necessity, they really can put up with most anything to make things happen. Maybe the universe just wanted to see if we were serious about finishing this trip."

Quebec proved to be their biggest challenge. Neither of them spoke French and the RV broke down. For two days, they sat in a parking lot frustrated at the vehicle, the language barrier, and their lack of funds. But eventually, they were back on the road, and headed toward their next market.

Even though they were well aware that they didn't have enough money to pay the fee for the three days of this market, they acknowledged that they had been taken care of so far, and *knew* that they weren't going to be stranded now. "Miracles happen when we persist in following our heart and don't give up," says Barb. Right on cue, the money flowed in, which gave them enough to head towards Prince Edward Island.

Exactly two months from the day they left their home, and 5467 miles later, they arrived at their son's home in Halifax. The first half of their dream had come true. On the shores of the Atlantic, their son built a cairn using west coast rock that Barb had brought, and poured Pacific waters into the Atlantic, uniting the west and east coasts. They spent eight days in Halifax, and in the process, ran out of money, then participated in more markets.

Labor Day weekend, they reluctantly headed homeward. In Ontario, heritage buildings and islands grabbed their attention. Prescott opened its arms, even sending the newspaper out to interview them. "It would appear that a couple of "Geriatric Gypsies" who are traveling on a dime and a dream are an unusual story. But then, why is it assumed that as people get older, they can't live out their dreams, too?" asks Barb.

They ran out of gas for the first time outside of Thunder Bay in the dark. Even this event produced "gifts of abundance" in the form of motorists who offered to help them, as well as a tow truck driver who gave them more gas than they had paid for.

Five markets in Thunder Bay brought more contacts for Dave's creations, and once again, they caught the attention of the local newspaper. A week later, they had enough money to head onward to Calgary, where the last of the driftwood was sold, which gave them the gas money they needed to get home.

110 days and 10,299 miles after they'd begun their trip, they

chugged their way back to the west coast. Being on a budget that had been dictated by how much they sold each day, they had to pay for campgrounds only four times during their entire trip. Mostly, they managed to stay for free in the parking lots of malls and truck stops.

Upon returning, they opened the door of their home and stood in wonder at what they'd just accomplished. They looked into each other's eyes and celebrated. They'd really done it; they had crossed Canada on a dime, and proved that dreams shouldn't be put off because of money.

Miracle Thinking Tips

- "Dream BIG for you can't stuff a great life into a small dream," says Barb. "The universe provides *if* we have faith. Miracles happen because we believe in them. In our hearts, we believed that people are inherently good, friendly and generous. That faith in our fellow man carried us over the 10,299 miles of our dream trip. When you believe, you open yourself up, and the miracles will then come from the most unexpected places. Take your dreams off the shelf and start living them."

- "Dreams require passionate persistence. Have unshakable faith in your dream, yourself, and your support system," she continues. "Tell everybody everywhere about your dream, for it will make you accountable. It will also make you into one big, walking, talking magnet and you will attract blessings from unforeseen places."

✦ Further, she says, "A dream without an action plan will stay just a dream. Know how to make it happen. Write it down often, as well as use visuals, to implant the dream in your heart. Also, give the universe something to bless." In her case, Barb used a little foam potato on which she wrote the words, Powell River to PEI, 2003 (Prince Edward Island). The little potato sat on her windowsill for a few years, teasing her every time she looked at it. The day they reached Prince Edward Island, she danced around the parking lot, with her foam potato in hand and sang, "We did it. We really, really did it!" The words on the potato had been fulfilled.

"I asked my hand for a message. "How is this injury serving me now?" The answer came quickly: "By being injured, you have nothing to risk."

– David Franklin

For Using Anger as a Guide for Healing . . .

'Digital' Alchemy

As a young teenager, the guitar was clearly David Franklin's favorite outlet for self-expression. Unlike the people in his life, music held no judgment, criticism or abuse. The guitar was his friend, the only constant in his world.

Although David enjoyed playing various forms of music, he particularly loved speed metal, with its loud, fast and aggressive pulse. Most of all, playing speed metal required a lot of endurance, as the style involved the ability to play in fast, downward picking movements using the right hand and arm. "To the observer, this style might look like a repetitive karate-chop set to warp-speed," says David.

David didn't just "play" the guitar; he "beat it up." Between practicing his speed metal music and playing tennis, his hand and arm received quite a workout, and within a few years, he developed such severe pain that playing either the guitar or tennis had become difficult. Although David wanted to go to college to pursue a career in music, now it was uncertain as to whether he'd even be able to play anymore.

Over the next eight years, he sought help from various doctors, including hand specialists, sports-medicine doctors, physical therapists and others. None of them could figure out what was wrong with his hand or heal his pain. One even accused him of faking the injury.

Totally frustrated, he switched fields, keeping the guitar as a hobby, as something he could do here and there whenever his hand felt up to it. Six years later, however, under the care of a chiropractor, David's hand and arm gradually improved. Although he thought he was healed for good, unfortunately, that was not to be the case.

A few more years passed and David decided to go back to school for a second degree, this time in music. While preparing to audition, his hand started to hurt again, just like it had years ago. Once more, he went to the doctors, and again, they were of no help. He figured it just wasn't in the cards for him to be a guitarist.

Several months later, though, while feeling sorry for himself, David began reflecting on his situation. During the past five years, he had been through counseling and had attended many personal growth workshops. In the process, he had released the anger he'd felt as a teenager.

On a spiritual and energetic level, David realized that his original injury had been due to the fact that he had been channeling all of his anger into his right arm. However, since he no longer felt that kind of anger anymore, he surmised that the injury must now be holding a different kind of meaning for him at this point in his life.

David asked his hand for a message. "How is this injury serving me now?" The answer came quickly: "By being injured, you have nothing to risk. You don't have to risk failing or risk not being good enough. You can be safe, comforted by your self-pity."

"I knew I had a choice," says David, "to stay safe, or to risk and be healed." As soon as David had this realization and acknowledged his choices, he felt a release in his hand and arm.

"Suddenly, I knew that my injury was gone and that I was healed," he says.

Six years have passed since David had this revelation. He has never once felt pain in his right arm or hand from that moment on.

"I am able to play and perform the music I love," he says, "although now, fortunately for my hand, it happens to be mostly classical music!"

Miracle Thinking Tips

- Understand that injuries and illnesses often occur when we experience an internal push/pull; we have a desire to have something – or someone – in our lives, and at the same time, we feel some sense of conflict (either consciously or subconsciously) about having this person or thing that we say we desire. David's desire was to be a professional guitarist. Yet, his underlying fear of failure led his subconscious to create a self-sabotaging injury to keep him "safe." If you are dealing with an injury or illness, check to see if there may be a conflicting push/pull underlying your circumstance as well.

✦ The key to David's healing involved his willingness to face the truth. "If you are willing to look deeper at your illness or injury than at what lies on the surface, you might discover vital information that could lead to your healing," says David, "Rather than seeing my injury solely on a physical level, I looked to its source as being a spiritual one." By believing the source of his injury held a deeper truth, and asking to hear that truth, David was able to quickly bring a chronic condition that had persisted for years to immediate resolution. "I took the time to reflect and be curious, and allowed the answers to come to me," he says. "When I tried desperately to find a solution, none came. When I stopped to listen and let an answer come, rather than dig for one, and surrendered, it came."

✦ If you've been given a dream, there will ultimately be a way for you to fulfill it, although the manner in which it is fulfilled, or the final result obtained may be different than what you imagined. "I stayed true to my dream," says David. "Even after seeing numerous doctors who were of no help, even after obtaining a degree that had nothing to do with music, and even after the injury returned, I still didn't give up. I stayed open to my dream coming true." If it's in your heart, stay the course.

*"Your miracles are small
until your faith expands.
Continue to expand your faith
daily, because if you can ask it,
your angels can deliver it."*

– Kathleen Ronald

For Growing a Business . . .

The Miracle Marketing Team

When Kathleen Ronald found herself floating amidst the rubble of the dotcom fallout, she initially decided to work three days a week as a marketing consultant. At the same time, she would slowly rebuild her speaking business over a two-year period. However, in praying for guidance, she received a message to focus her energy entirely on her speaking career and not go back to the marketing position at all.

Yikes! Could her speaking career match the kind of income she was used to making in the corporate world? Kathleen had serious doubts. Feeling overwhelmed with fear, she decided she'd better have a conversation with God and her angels fast.

"Look!" she said, "If I'm going to do this, then you'd better make that phone ring. You'd better handle the details and bring me the big contracts I'm used to!" Through tears, she heard the reply, "We've just been waiting for you."

And so her journey began . . . For the first eight months, she focused on creating the perfect web site. However, since she had spent so much time focusing on that one area, she hadn't created a sales or marketing plan. At one point, feeling overwrought with this new business that she wasn't even entirely sure about, she decided to call on her angels once again. This time, her conversation went something like this ...

"Booking Angels, I need you now! Show me the money!"

Shortly thereafter, she received a phone call in which she was invited to lead a training at a conference. There was just one problem: she didn't lead the kind of training the person had called about. However, by the end of that phone call, she was invited to present her training anyway.

Arriving at the conference, the time slot for her presentation couldn't have been any worse – the last day of a four-day event ... after lunch. Only twenty people had registered. Kathleen offered a prayer: "Lord, whoever is going be there is exactly who needs to be there. So whoever could be blessed by using my products or services, have them come to my class."

The numbers gradually grew. Says Kathleen, "In faith, I told the event producer, 'we should set up the room for seventy because I'm expecting standing room only." The result? Seventy people attended Kathleen's course, which also ended up being the number one rated training that year out of a field of fifty presenters.

That event led to the next, then the next. Five years later, Kathleen's business continues to snowball. She considers her business her 'ministry' and maintains a prayer list in her head of places where she wants to speak. She tells her angels, "When it's time for me to do my ministry there, then you make the arrangements."

To attract business when she attends trade shows or networking events, she doesn't frantically pace the floor looking to drum up new clients. Instead, she says a simple prayer she learned from author, Doreen Virtue: "Dear Lord, please bless me with all the people who would be blessed by using my products and services and have them find me at this event today. For this I pray and say, 'Thank you.' Amen." Having asked for the right connections to find her, she walks into a room fully expecting to enjoy herself and have fun.

Says Kathleen, "My heart is open. I can just give freely. There's no manipulation, there's no planning, there's no goal. My only goal is to let God do His thing. When friends suggest we go here, or do this or that in order to get business, I tell them, 'No. We're going to stand here at this table and people will come to us.' You don't have to go knock your brains out."

Miracle Thinking Tips

* Says Kathleen, "Your miracles are small until your faith expands. Continue to expand your faith daily, because if you can ask it, your angels can deliver it."

* "Let God and the angels orchestrate everything. Let them be your business partners. They will even manage your calls and appointments. If you want quiet, ask them to hold your calls. There's nothing they won't do. You can also call on specific angels for help. For example, you can call on your writing angels, your comprehension angels, or your financial angels – whatever you need."

* Miracle Thinkers embrace the power of prayer. Al-

though she says she still doesn't have time for marketing, she makes time every day to 'have counsel with a million angels.' "To pray, be specific and include all the things you want. Pray before you get on the phone, go to a meeting, or get in the car. Always pray for the outcome that you're looking for, then release it, and say 'thank you.' Then the best outcome happens."

"To receive all of the good things in life, be loving and forgiving toward yourself."

– Robert Plath

Starting a Global Movement

"I hope you drop dead!" Thirteen-year-old, Robert Plath, would never have dared to speak those words out loud to the man who made every day of his existence more miserable than the last. Instead, he muttered the words silently to himself, while enduring yet another slap to his head or strapping from his father. Then one day, quite suddenly, his father reeled over from a heart attack, thereby accommodating the young man's wishes.

Robert's first thoughts were, "Good. I'll be the boss. I'll have mother. I'll have the car..." Then pretty quickly, overwhelming feelings of guilt began to seep into his conscience. Would his father be alive today if he hadn't secretly wished him dead? Had he caused his father's death?

The guilt Robert felt plagued him for years. However, having been raised in a tough Detroit neighborhood, Robert had been taught from an early age to never show his emotions. "When I was a little kid in the back yards of Detroit, I was taught a war role model," says Robert. "I learned that I was one of the 'good guys' and that some of the others were the 'bad guys.' My friends and I would throw tin cans and mud bombs filled with apples at the 'bad guys.' It was wrong to show your feelings, and you had to be tough. If you got hurt, you could never cry." Stuffing the guilt into the far recesses of his mind, he grew up, obtained a degree in law, and eventually moved to California.

As an adult, Robert began attending personal growth seminars. Feeling buoyed by the unconditional love he received from his fellow participants at these workshops, little by little, he was able to release the stifled guilt, anger and sadness that had accompanied him through most of his life.

Forgiveness, however, was still another matter. Although Robert could forgive his father in workshop settings, at other times, the anger he felt toward this man would feel just as real as it had in his adolescence. Eventually, Robert came to the realization that the only way he could create lasting happiness was to learn how to forgive. And who better to learn from than those who had mastered the act?

In 1996, Robert founded the Worldwide Forgiveness Alliance, and created International Forgiveness Day, which takes place the first Sunday of August each year. "On Forgiveness Day, we honor 'Heroes and Champions of Forgiveness, Reconciliation and Peace,'" says Robert, who invites individuals who have endured the most difficult of experiences, yet have embraced the healing power of forgiveness, to share their stories.

"I wanted to provide role models for kids," says Robert, who is also creating forgiveness programs for schools. "I choose people who I consider to be truly heroic, truly genuine – including guys who have been into all kinds of trouble and who have been deeply hurt, but who have worked their way through it."

As a thirteen-year-old, when Robert looked at a picture of himself at age three, the image that stared back at him was of a little boy who was "a wreck. There was no joy in my face," says Robert. Now, every day, Robert wakes up excited about what might happen next.

"I got a call from Ghana at 4 in the morning telling me they're going to celebrate International Forgiveness Day. Then I got a letter from Nigeria, where there are 130 million people, and they're doing a Forgiveness Day. Recently, a veteran called me who wants to get all of the veterans who have fought in all of the wars to do a silent forgiveness vigil together. If we were to have a silent vigil with all those veterans from all those wars on Forgiveness Day each year, it would be colossal."

Miracle Thinking Tips

* "Forgiveness has a power to it," says Robert. "It represents a form of freedom. When you forgive, you have an ability to pick up on the needs of others – their fears, their humanity, their vulnerability. You gain insight and empathy, and as you get these new insights about yourself and what happened in your past, somehow there is a shift that begins, which allows you to see yourself in a different way. This is what I call forgiveness."

* "Studies by Dr. Luskin at Stanford University indicate that forgiveness heals by reducing stress,"

says Robert. "Heart attacks can come from anger. I handed out a flyer showing the health aspects of forgiveness to a man who had suffered from two heart attacks in six months. He'd been having huge battles with his two sons. After we talked, he said, 'I'm going to go make two phone calls right now.' Three weeks later, I saw this man and he looked entirely different. He said, 'I got together with my sons and we totally resolved everything. I feel so great.' He was a transformed man."

✻ "How you do in every aspect of your life stems from how loving and forgiving you are toward yourself. If you don't forgive yourself, you are not going to feel good about yourself. If you are not feeling good about yourself, you're not going to allow yourself to have all that you could have or be the greatness that you are." To receive all of the good things in life, be loving and forgiving toward yourself.

"Put yourself first. There's an incredible energy that arises in us when we can speak the truth."

– Steven Walters

For Situations Involving Life and Death . . .

Choosing Life

Having been told he had only 24 hours left to live, the family of Steven Walters solemnly gathered around the bedside of the young man who was barely clinging to life. Although he had leukemia, the doctors weren't sure if he might die first from cardiac arrest due to his heart's increasingly erratic flutter, or the pneumonia, which was rapidly suffocating the breath out of his lungs.

Accepting his inevitable fate, Steven intended to be a "good die'er." He decided that he would deliver a sweet goodbye to all those present, and make sure they were okay before he left. Meanwhile, with the oxygen mask delivering 100% oxygen to his lungs, he could hardly speak.

Then something quite inexplicable happened; gradually, a sense of awareness came over Steven that made him feel as though he still had some inkling of choice as to whether he stayed or passed. In the slightest whisper, he signaled his older brother to have everybody leave the room.

When everyone was gone, intuitively, Steven felt that he needed to sit up, so he asked his brother to raise the bed. This simple action, which no doctor had ever suggested, allowed his lungs to receive more oxygen. The feeling of suffocation subsided.

Next, Steven felt the impulse to meditate, so he closed his eyes. He thought of his old swim coach from his days in high school. "See if you can find just 10% more oxygen," reminded the coach. Steven breathed very slowly and deeply. For close to two hours, he stayed in that position. Eventually, he felt enveloped by a sense of inner stillness. Even his pounding heart responded by slowing down to a normal rate.

At the end of his meditation, he leaned back, totally exhausted. As he drifted into sleep, he realized that he might not wake up again. However, hours later when he did awaken, he started the breathing and meditating process all over again. Within a week, the young man who had been given 24 hours to live was released from the hospital.

Shortly thereafter, a doctor in New Jersey was suggested to Steven. Although he had a fibrosis in his bone marrow – which all his doctors had told him couldn't be treated – this new doctor informed him about a hospital that had been successfully performing this kind of bone marrow transplant for a few years. Within days, Steven was on a plane to Seattle.

Luckily, Steven's brother Mark was a perfect match for his marrow, which meant Steven wouldn't need radiation, although the chemo he would endure would be very intense. However, Steven recovered beautifully, and more than ten years have passed since his harrowing ordeal.

Miracle Thinking Tips

- ✳ You are in charge. One of the keys to Miracle Thinking is to feel your power. Even if the world is falling down around you or things don't go the way you want, you can take control over some aspect of your life. For example, Steven put up a sign on his hospital door that read, "Do not disturb. Meditating." This allowed him to meditate without interruption. "I needed space by myself," says Steven. "Every other day, I was allowed to take a bath. They'd unplug me from everything. I would sit in the bath, in total quiet, and find my own stillness, my own place inside. It was my way of running it the way I needed to."

- ✳ Miracle Thinkers do the most compassionate thing for themselves. "When we take care of ourselves in the moment, we're not coddling or patronizing anybody, and most importantly, we're not fooling ourselves about what's okay. Stop being a nice guy. Put yourself first," says Steven. For example, a nurse whom he really liked injected fluids too forcefully into a line that had been inserted into his chest, which completely stopped his flow of oxygen. There was no more air and he was suffocating. Later that day, the nurse said, "I'm so sorry. I'd still like to care for you if it's okay with you." However, it wasn't okay with Steven. Even though she was very sweet, Steven realized he no longer implicitly trusted her. Although it was difficult to say 'no,' Steven realized that with everything he was going through he didn't need the added stress.

✦ Tell the absolute truth. Says Steven, "My truth came out like a laser during this experience. It was another side of my healing to see that I have the power to choose, and to say what's okay and what's not okay. There's an incredible energy that arises in us when we can speak the truth. The more I can say those difficult things that need to be said, the quicker I can let them go. As Ramana Maharshi taught: 'Let what comes come. Let what goes go. Find out what remains.'"

"Anger repels wealth. If there is anger within your soul, you are repelling money whether you know it or not."

– Suze Orman

For Financial Abundance...

Anger Repels Wealth

(Author Story)

In an interview with Suze Orman, the country's foremost woman-whiz of moolah-management once shared quite an intriguing statement with me: "Anger repels wealth." Says Suze, "If there is anger within your soul, you are repelling money whether you know it or not."

She experienced this principal first-hand while stuck in a traffic jam. From her limo, she noticed a man perched on a piece of cardboard asking passersby for cigarettes. Everyone ignored him. Suze decided to give him all the money in her purse – which totaled seventy dollars – and really make his day.

However, just as she was about to exit the limo, he spat at the next couple who walked by. She sat back down in her seat and closed her purse. "This man didn't know I was in the car watching him," says Suze. "He did not know that seventy dollars was about to come his way. But as soon as I saw him spit, I told my driver to drive on. I did not get out of the car, and I did not give him the seventy dollars. His anger repelled the money that was about to come his way, and he didn't even know it . . ."

The moral? Don't spit at people. <wink>

Miracle Thinking Tips

- Miracle Thinkers understand that unresolved emotions such as anger, resentment, frustration, disappointment, jealousy and envy, block the flow of their Highest Good. When Miracle Thinkers feel a simmering feeling, they take positive steps to move that feeling out of their thoughts and out of their body. To do so, they might just observe the feeling and try to establish its location in their body. They might focus on their breath, or go for a walk, or pound a pillow. Often, they journal or write a letter of forgiveness, which may or may not be sent. Some might see a therapist. Choose an activity that helps you to attain a neutral state.

- Ida Fourman, my beloved grandmother, was a Miracle Thinker. She used to say, "It's better to light a candle then to curse the darkness." Therefore, Miracle Thinkers wish good things for themselves rather, then spending time brooding or thinking ill of others. If a Miracle Thinker starts to feel envious of another's good fortune, they make it a point to lavish blessings upon that person instead. As one extends blessings to another, blessings will be coming your way as well.

- Miracle Thinkers also understand that nobody's life
  – regardless of how much money, fame or love they
  appear to have – plays out like a fairy tale, and that
  our love is always needed.

"Bless a person who has triggered you, and you will quickly feel released from him and his drama. Ask that he be shown his next highest step."

– Reverend Delorise Lucas

For Overcoming Those Curve Balls Life Throws Your Way

How I Found Happiness by Working for Embezzlers

(Author Story)

I had just been hired as the chief freelance writer for a new national magazine and the pay was phenomenal.

First monkey wrench: The day I was supposed to be issued my big fat, juicy paycheck for the six months of work I'd given my blood, sweat, and typing fingers to, I receive a notice informing me that there had been a slight delay. Alarmed, I called the senior editor.

"We're having some unexpected concerns, but we're all praying, and we're sure the angels will find a way to pay you."

Thought bubble above my head: Angels? What? You mean there's no business plan?

Second monkey wrench: My sinking feeling was confirmed a few weeks later when the company was placed under investigation by the FBI. How was I supposed to know the angels they chose to pray to were the Angels of Embezzlement?

On my personal Richter Scale, this was a disaster of monumental proportions. Like a dog chasing its tail, I desperately tried to reach the "Kick Me" sign on my back and rip it off. However, not being able to reach it, I instead resigned myself to slinking in misery.

To quell my pathetic wallowing, the following day I wandered into a local music store, since music has always been one of the ways in which I take refuge. Offhandedly, I inquired as to whether there were any southpaw guitars. In response, I was led to the "expensive" room, where I was shown a beauty of a guitar. Never an impulse buyer, the second my hands hit the strings, I knew this was my guitar. I HAD to have this guitar.

"How much is it?" I asked.

Third monkey wrench: "$1000," came the reply.

Looking the sales clerk straight in the eye, I declared, "I am going to own this guitar within a month." Even though I didn't have the money, I knew with absolute certainty that this was my guitar, and that somehow, I would own this guitar within a month.

The next day, when I mentioned the guitar to a friend, she said, "Why don't you hold a performance and ask all your friends to prepay for tickets? That way you can buy the guitar beforehand and play it at the show."

Images of a young Mickey Rooney with lots of adolescent freckles flashed through my mind … "Hey kids! Let's put on a show in the barn!" It was a great idea. There was just one problem …

Fourth monkey wrench: I dreaded performing. However, I wanted this guitar so much that I found myself saying 'yes.' When another friend offered her house as a venue for my debut, I quickly sent off an email invitation to my circle of friends and acquaintances, asking for contributions of $20 or more to support me in creating my dream guitar. Mission accomplished, I then turned my mind to the creation of the performance.

I didn't want to play my guitar the entire time. That was just too scary. Since it had been my lifelong dream to be a published author, I decided I might as well read some stories from my manuscript, too. Over the following month, my mind also whipped up some comical skits to add to the mix.

First miracle: In all, sixty-four generous people responded to my invitation, and the week prior to the show, I held $1200 in my hand.

Second miracle: When I raced down to the store to purchase my dream guitar, the clerk greeted me with some unexpected news: "We just discovered that this is a used guitar. It's on consignment. We'll sell it to you for $450."

Third miracle: The huge reduction in price allowed me to purchase a microphone, a mic stand, a guitar case, and a special effects unit, as well as pay for the church hall I'd rented when my ticket sales had outgrown my friend's house. Happily, I rushed home and proceeded to play up a storm to practice for my big debut.

Finally, the night of the show arrived. Inwardly, I was terrified. However, being doggedly determined to see it through, I plugged the guitar into the amplifier to do a sound check. Dead silence. Quick! Fool with knobs. More silence. Try a different cord! No difference; there was a short in the electronic part of the guitar.

Now, where had this giant monkey wrench come from? First, the embezzlers and no pay for six months of work, then all the energy I'd put into creating this special event, and now the amplification for the guitar was broken and 64 people were about to walk through the door. Distraught, I dissolved into a pile of tears.

One of my friends who had arrived early listened to my lament. "Why can't things be easy?" I squeaked out through giant sobs.

"I know what you mean. Remember, my house burnt down last week," was her response.

(Darn! I was just one-upped. Even in my worst despair, there was someone in that moment who could one-up me! Can't I just have my own little lousy moment)?

Fourth miracle: Even without amplification, the show was a whopping success. In fact, it was so much fun that I moved beyond my fear of being on-stage and created two more full-length shows called, "Comic Intervention for Closet Visionaries and Almost Manifesters."

The biggest miracle of all: One day, while I was shopping my manuscript at a publishing convention, I started schmoozing with a publisher and happened to mention my one-woman show.

"A show?" Her right eyebrow raised a notch. "Tell me about it."

The publisher loved the idea that I was doing a show because that meant that I was visible in the world, and visibility is the key to book sales. In that moment, six years of frustration and disappointment, as potential publishers had beckoned then disappeared, ended. I procured a signed contract in two week's time and was able to begin my lifelong dream of being an author.

The truth is, if I hadn't worked for embezzlers I never would have created a show, and if I hadn't created a show, I would probably still be looking for a publisher today. However, because of that whole experience, I wound up being able to manifest my dream, and my first book, *Crappy to Happy,* launched my career as an author.

Miracle Thinking Tips

* When we are in the midst of a difficult life circumstance, it is often impossible to anything good can be gained from the horrible mess we find ourselves in. We might feel victimized and powerless. It then becomes very easy to recite the woes of our lives to anyone who will listen. However, the constant repetition of our hard luck story only enforces the power of that story to rule our lives. Miracle Thinkers understand that the story is just a story. They know that they have the power to rewrite their story by taking action steps. Action steps help Miracle Thinkers to take back their power whenever they feel victimized.

* A Bolivian shaman, named Chamalu, once said, "In my country, we pray for difficult people to enter our lives because they are our greatest teachers." Miracle Thinkers have learned that betrayers, bullies, and backstabbers are often brought into our lives to strengthen us or to help us stretch in some significant way.

* Miracle Thinkers discover that it's never worth it to carry anger and pain onward. As Reverend Delorise Lucas often said: "The sooner you can bless a person who has triggered you, the quicker you will feel released from them and their drama." "Free yourself and forgive yourself. Then forgive them by asking

in prayer that these difficult people be shown their next highest step. Once you've asked that they be shown their next highest step, release them. Let them go. Move on. You've got better things to do with your precious life."

"Have you had enough joy?"
said the voice from the other
side. "Well, no. I'm only 30," I
replied. "What are you waiting
for?" said the voice.

– Dawna Markova

An Angel in the Darkness

During her first long hospital stay, Dawna Markova, then in her early thirties, was facing a medical procedure for cancer that terrified her. Late one night, she heard a swishing sound coming from the hallway. The sound came closer until it stopped in front of her door. Looking up, she saw a rather large woman pushing a mop. The woman entered her room, and plopped herself into the chair by her bedside in a way that one does when they are in the company of an old friend.

Without saying a word, the woman reached over and put her hand on Dawna's ankle and began to breathe in unison with her. As Dawna closed her eyes, she imagined the woman's breath sounded like ocean waves washing back and forth against the shore. A while later, the woman stood up and grabbed her broom. Before she left, she turned and said in her thick Jamaican accent, "You're more than your pain." Then she was gone.

All day long, Dawna questioned herself, "How could I be

more than my pain? In processing this question, she thought about how her pain didn't cover her entire body. Truthfully, only 20% of her body was in pain. Logically, didn't that mean that 80% of her body wasn't in pain? She decided to just take notice of that fact, instead of putting all of her attention on the source of her discomfort.

The next night, Dawna heard the familiar swishing sound of the mop coming down the hallway. Once again, the woman re-appeared and proceeded to collapse into the chair as she reached for Dawna's foot. The comfort Dawna received from the woman's loving presence felt palpable. Then the woman said, "You're more than the sickness in that body."

Every night, her "Jamaican angel" would appear, collapse in the chair beside her, and place her hand on her foot as Dawna lay silently in the bed. Dawna stopped taking her bedtime morphine just to make sure she wasn't hallucinating. The night of her last visit, the woman said, "You're not the fear in that body. You're more than that fear. Float on it. Float above it." Then she left.

"What does it mean to be more than one's fear?" Dawna asked herself. Eventually, she arrived at an answer. Of course! Her capacity for joy was so much greater than her fear. Instead of focusing her attention on anything that made her feel fearful, Dawna decided to focus only on those things that brought her joy.

Dawna never saw her "Jamaican angel" again. Was she really an angel, or just the nighttime cleaning lady? To Dawna, it never really mattered. This kind being provided a deep and abiding sense of loving comfort to a woman who was in great fear and pain, and by doing so, had inspired Dawna to focus her attention in a new way that changed her perspective.

Still dealing with the cancer a few years later, Dawna had another experience in which she was pronounced dead on an operating table. While being wheeled to the morgue, she felt as though she was 'falling upward.'

"During this time which felt timeless, all the questions I'd ever asked and all the experiences I'd ever had came together," she says. "I had the comprehension that I was light, that I was love, and that love cannot be destroyed, whether or not you're in a body."

As she watched from above, the doctor came out of the operating room and delivered the difficult news to her eight-year-old son, David.

"In my experience, there was a one-way wall, and the wall was only on David's side," says Dawna. "This wall was made up of his anger, his fear, and his belief that I was dead. But I wasn't! My love and my consciousness were right there. I knew everything that was happening to him."

"I also comprehended how incomplete my loving had been to him," she continued. "There were many lessons I hadn't yet learned at that point. I understood that David would suffer as a result. All I wanted was to get through to David so that I could help him not suffer from my incomplete lessons. But I couldn't get through because of that wall of his belief."

Next, a voice began to engage her in conversation. It asked, "Have you had enough joy?"

She responded, "Well, no. I'm only thirty years old."

"What are you waiting for?" said the voice.

Then the voice asked, "What's unfinished for you to give?"

"What do you mean? I want a Ferrari, and I want my own house . . ."

The question was repeated over and over again, "What's unfinished for you to give?"

Upon her return after 4-1/2 minutes of being pronounced dead, Dawna's understanding of the meaning of her life deepened dramatically. Most importantly, her focus shifted from a desire to 'get,' to a desire to 'give.'

The author of numerous books, Dawna approached her publisher and originated the idea for the "Random Acts of Kindness" books, which have propelled thousands of people across the planet to give of themselves to others.

Miracle Thinking Tips

- "Fear can either be an ending to one's growth and dreams or a beginning," says Dawna. Being aware of my passion, for example, gave fear a companion, someone to hold it as if the Madonna were holding an infant. Do not ignore fear. Rather, notice it as a sensation in the body. By caring about it, and then by shifting your focus to what is more than your fear, the energy is released to move forward."

- "When you're going through an experience of fear or anxiety, you can ask yourself, 'What is it that brings me joy?' and begin to focus on your joy. The bigger your joy, the smaller your fear will be. It's not that the fear will go away; it's just that it will become less and less relevant. The joy will carry you forward."

✦ As a Miracle Thinker, it's important to understand the following distinction that Dawna makes: "Don't confuse joy with pleasure. Joy is about the connection that comes when you've given of yourself. For example, when you deeply connect with yourself, another, or nature, you experience joy. Pleasure, on the other hand, is about receiving, not about giving. For example, a therapeutic massage can bring pleasure, but I've found that my fear is not bigger than that. If I think in terms of pleasure, it's never bigger than my fear. When I see my infant granddaughter's eyes light up at her first taste of ice cream – that's joy."

"The Universe will never give you a 'yes . . . but.' No matter what kind of miracle you want to create, you must get off your 'but.'"

– Randy Peyser

Fairy Tales Do Come True *(Author Story)*

Tilting past my mid-forties, I yearned for a loving, happy relationship that would last decades longer than my car payments. However, when it came to flunking relationships, after thirty years of practice, I was a pro. I had become a true master of what some might term, "the accelerated path to growth," meaning, those brief, intense relationships that leave skewer marks across your heart while enabling you to work out your mother or father issues, or learn some particular lesson that your soul needed to learn, before you can have the relationship you truly desire.

After years of continual disappointment, I didn't really believe that it was possible for me to actually have a lasting relationship. I thought that others could have it, but for some reason, I couldn't and never would. I'd followed the advice of my peers and read all the books. I'd made a list of the qualities I'd wanted in a partner and tacked it up above my bed as a prayer to God. But months later, when the words, "still single," could have been accurately tattooed on my forehead, I ripped the list off the wall, crumpled it up and threw it in the waste basket, thoroughly disgusted.

One night, a question emerged among a group of friends. "Where is your edge?" In the course of that conversation, I realized that what I wanted the most was a relationship. Yet, what did I fear the most? Of course – a relationship. It became crystal clear – after years of disastrous relationships, I desperately feared the thing that I claimed I wanted the most. Therefore, while I was beckoning the Universe to fulfill my desires on one hand, subconsciously, I was pleading with the Universe not to fulfill my desires on the other hand. Under these conditions, the Universe could not fulfill my dream.

How could I turn this situation around? Instead of going to therapy to resolve the years of fears I had obviously been schlepping along with me, I closed my eyes, and in my heart of hearts, asked myself the question: "What is it that I am truly willing to allow?"

An answer bubbled up: "I'm willing to allow a phone call with someone new." I thought about it some more. "I'm willing to allow a dinner with someone new." Eventually, I added, "I'm willing to allow holding hands with a new person – maybe." That was as far as I could take it, and that was all right with me. By paying attention to my answers to that question, I would stay in my truth in each moment and only do what I truly felt comfortable doing.

It had been six years since I'd been in a relationship. With this new strategy, however, I attracted a new person to myself almost immediately. And was it my dream partner? Absolutely not. In fact, it was actually the worst relationship of my life. However, because of the circumstances surrounding that rather brief, but embroiled, encounter, I moved to another town where events were lining up for me to meet a very different person. Less than two weeks after that terrible relationship evaporated, I met my true life-partner and we've been together ever since.

Miracle Thinking Tips

- Miracle Thinkers understand that the Universe will wholeheartedly respond to a "yes." The Universe will not respond to a yes/no or a yes/but. If you want to find your soul mate or create whatever it is that your heart most desires, you must be able to say 'yes' to that desire, completely and without any sense of hesitation.

- To achieve your "yes," I've created a practice called, The "Ruth IRA," that can help. (My middle name is Ruth). Unlike the Roth IRA, which entails setting aside money for your retirement, think of the Ruth IRA as a method to help you set aside your objections to making your dreams come true. IRA is an acronym. The "I" in the Ruth IRA stands for "Insistence." Miracle Thinkers insist! One night, I had a dream in which the letters I-N-S-I-S-T were spelled out on a Scrabble board. Immediately upon awakening, I asked myself, "What is it that I want so much that I am absolutely willing to insist that it happen?" I realized that whatever it was that I was absolutely willing to insist upon was what I could create in this lifetime. The same applies to you; whatever it is that you are absolutely willing to insist upon is what you can create in your life.

✦ The "R" in the Ruth IRA stands for "Resistance." When we say we want something, but find ourselves pushing our good away either consciously or subconsciously through our fears or feelings of unworthiness, we are in resistance. If you can think of any downside to having what it is you say you want, you've got some degree of resistance to work through. For example, I truly wanted a relationship, but at the same time, I had so much fear from having been hurt in the past that it was impossible for me to receive a loving relationship.

✦ *The key:* The "A" in the Ruth IRA stands for "Allowing." When you want something but can't quite insist upon it because some degree of resistance is present, ask yourself, *"What is it that I am truly willing to allow?"* By listening to your heart and staying in your own truth in every moment, you will allow what is true for you to keep emerging, without feeling the need to push it away. You will never get more than you can handle when you ask yourself, *"What is it that I am truly willing to allow?"* Listen deeply to your own inner answers.

"Specific sounds cause brain wave shifts. When the brain, heart and breath shift, the entire physiology of the body changes."

– Debra LeForest

For Understanding the Healing Power of Creativity . . .

Creativity Sends Cancer Packing

Debra LeForest landed in the Bay Area and found herself living in a semi-converted garage, which was attached to the rental home of someone she hardly knew. It was her hope to quickly find employment and create a more suitable living situation. One afternoon, the phone rang in the house. Although she had never answered this woman's phone before, for some reason she found herself picking up the receiver and engaging in a conversation with the stranger who had called to speak with the woman.

When Debra casually mentioned her need for employment to this stranger, she was given a possible resource to call, and as a result, within one day, she was hired to help coordinate a conference related to alternative medicine. Relieved, she began her new temporary employment. However, the conference failed to bring in the amount of attendance that was necessary to fund an event of such large proportions, and the sponsors wound up offering Debra a partial trade of health care in lieu of money.

Disappointed, she decided she might as well take the docs up on their offer, since they wouldn't be able to pay her the full amount they owed her anyway.

Before she went to her appointment, she called the stranger on the phone, who by this time was becoming her friend. The stranger said, "I had a dream about you last night. I dreamt you had golf balls in your mouth."

To Debra's surprise, upon examining her mouth, the doctors discovered a pre-cancerous condition, called leukoplakia. Filled with anxiety, Debra lay in bed for three days, and fasted and prayed while thinking about why she would have this condition in her mouth. Finally, she asked her Higher Self, "Why do I have this condition?"

The answer came to her – she needed to be creative again. This was the universe's way of getting her attention. It was true. Long ago, she had packed up her guitar and had stopped singing. She realized that she had been blocking her creativity for a long time.

She found a furnished cabin in the woods to sublet. It just so happened that the cabin was set up with the occupant's musical recording equipment, which he gave Debra permission to use while he spent the summer surfing in Hawaii.

Dusting off the cobwebs from her twelve-string guitar, Debra played her heart out, recording each note as they issued forth. For ten days, she did nothing but sing, play and record. She even invited the stranger on the phone, who was also a guitarist, to play with her. Once again, her creativity was freely flowing.

At the end of ten days, when Debra returned to the doctor's office, the leukoplakia had entirely disappeared.

Fascinated by the healing power of music that she had just experienced, Debra went on to study the therapeutic effects of sound wave frequencies. She created an instrumental music tape for relaxation called, "HeavenScent," with the stranger, who happens to be me – the author of this book. She also became one of the first – if not the first – sound therapists in the country to be employed in an alternative medical clinic and a health spa, where she generates healing sound frequencies through a vibroacoustic table to clients in need of relief from a wide range of symptoms.

Miracle Thinking Tips

* Explore your creativity. Debra advises, "The creative process is healing because it reminds us of our Divine Nature and that we are connected to a Higher Source, the All That Is. When you remember this sacred part of yourself and that you are connected to a Higher Source, the universe will flow through you and anything is possible."

* Listen to music designed for therapeutic purposes. "Certain sounds can facilitate us to bypass the mind and enter into that realm that is beyond the mind," says Debra. "Specific sounds can also cause body systems to change, first by manipulating the brain waves, causing brain wave shifts. The brain then tells the heart rhythms to shift, and then the breath follows in suit. When the brain, heart and breath shift, the entire physiology of the body will change.

✦ The path to a goal is rarely a straight line. If Debra hadn't picked up the phone, she wouldn't have found out about the stranger's contact in the alternative medical world and wouldn't have worked for the conference. If the conference had achieved maximum attendance, she would have been paid and would never have had an appointment with the doctor. Without the appointment with the doctor, she might not have discovered the pre-cancerous condition. If she hadn't discovered the pre-cancerous condition, she might never have discovered that she needed to be in her creative flow. If she hadn't been in her creative flow, she might never have discovered the healing power of sound and music, which launched her career in a new direction.

"Instead of saying, 'I've got some bad news,' try saying, 'I've got a miracle in the making.'"

– Randy Peyser

For Turning a Potential Disaster into a Miracle . . .

Plumbing for Miracles
(Author Story)

As first time homebuyers, my partner and I had recently purchased a highly overpriced, postage stamp of a house in California. Fortunately, the tiny house was in immaculate condition,
even at 41 years of age. However, two weeks after moving in, the
kitchen sink backed up and stubbornly refused to drain.

As my partner left for work, I called in our first line of home
defense – a friend who was a handyman of sorts – and within
an hour, he determined that the problem was more complicated
than we'd first thought. So I called the Home Warranty company,
who quickly dispatched a plumber.

The plumber climbed up on the roof to snake a pipe, and
three hours later declared that either a foreign object was stuck
in the pipe or there was a wrong fitting that was preventing the
snake from going all the way through.

I almost fell over when he delivered his prognosis: "You need
to call in a carpenter to rip out the back wall of your house so I

can get to the pipe." The approximate cost: $1000. This is the kind of news a new homeowner does not want to hear. Of course, this job would not be covered by the Home Warranty we'd so eagerly purchased in order to feel secure when household problems, such as this one, occurred.

I debated how to break the bad news to my partner. "Well honey, I've got some really bad news . . . " or "Sit down, you're not going to want to hear this . . . " or "Guess what I found out today?" None of these options gave me a good feeling as I visualized my partner wincing upon hearing the verdict.

Then an idea came to mind: what if I held this event as a miracle in the making, even though I couldn't predict the outcome? This seemed like a reasonable option to explore. So, when my partner arrived home, instead of saying, "I've got some really bad news," I said, "We've got a miracle in the making."

After sharing the plumber's assessment, we decided that we would both hold the intention that this situation was a miracle in the making. We knew a plumber who attended a weekly Course in Miracles group we sometimes frequented, so we gave him a call. The next afternoon, he fixed the problem within fifteen minutes, using a one-of-a-kind snake he'd devised to fit into small drains like ours. He didn't even charge us. No ripped out wall. No $1000 unexpected expense. No aggravation. Just a true miracle in the making.

Miracle Thinking Tips

✦ Miracle Thinkers decide what they want the outcome of any experience to be, regardless of the appearance of circumstances. Instead of staying focused on the idea that the only way to solve this situation would have been to rip out the wall, we first decided to view this situation as a miracle in the making. Did holding this frame of reference influence the outcome? You bet it did.

* Miracle Thinkers set intentions. Before we called our friend, the plumber, we stated an intention to the Universe: "We ask that Johnny come out tomorrow and fix our drain easily and effortlessly." The next day, we received the exact outcome we'd intended.

* Miracle Thinkers stay open to new options that are yet unknown. Did we have to know all the answers to create our miracle? No, we only knew one person who was a plumber, so we called him. However, what are the odds that our plumber friend would have the exact tool – which he had invented – to repair our specific problem? If we'd stayed with the 'bad news' story, and called any other plumber, the back of our house would have looked like a giant cat door with a big gaping hole in it. However, by shifting our focus of attention from the "bad news story" to the "miracle in the making story," we allowed a miracle to come to us.

"God cannot be limited, therefore our experience need not be limited."

– Christine Hodil

Moving on Faith

What do you do when Spirit tells you it's time to recreate your life somewhere else? Being highly intuitive, when Christine Hodil felt the urge from Spirit to move to Mt. Shasta after having spent many years in the Bay Area, she headed up the highway to investigate her options. Logically, such a move made no sense, but trusting the voice of Spirit, she knew with certainty that she had to go.

After consulting various friends and the local papers, she arrived in the Shasta area on a holiday weekend, where all she could find was a temporary sublet in a condominium complex. Intuitively, she sensed that this sublet would be noisy, but the woman who lived in the condo assured Christine that her place was perfectly quiet. When Christine moved in, however, it was, indeed, perfectly noisy due to a deaf neighbor who had invited one of his deaf friends to stay at his home.

Although the two were rather noisy, the owner desired to be considerate. Unfortunately, he unexpectedly went on vacation, leaving his friend in charge of his place. Soon afterwards, the noise level increased tremendously, and trash and broken items began to appear in the front yard.

After having been repeatedly disturbed by this man's raucous rackets, one day, at 3:30 in the morning, Christine called the police to report that the neighbor's friend was out in the yard playing a conga drum. When the officer came to her door, he told her that the man had just been incarcerated for disturbing the peace at several locations. He had been let out of jail, however, because there was not enough room to hold him.

Acknowledging that the man was obviously mentally unbalanced, and not being able to do anything further since he had quieted down by the time the police arrived, the officer left Christine alone to wonder if the man, in his recklessness, might burn down the condo while he smoked, or even if he might become violent toward her.

In a state of anguish, Christine decided she needed to view her experience from an entirely different angle. Perhaps she was calling this experience forth from Spirit as a lesson she needed, or perhaps this inappropriate character was providing her with an opportunity to learn something or heal something within herself. Quietly, she acknowledged this possibility by stating, "Okay God, this is about me. Am I going to run away or not?"

She started to pray and eventually came to a place of acceptance; the situation was what it was, and it was okay exactly the way it was. Says Christine, "I relaxed into the Love that always surrounds me and felt comforted. From that vantage point, "I asked my inner guidance if I was in danger, no matter what it looked like from the outside. Intuitively, I could feel that the guy was going to be quiet, and most likely, just go to sleep. As I allowed myself to open to this bigger Love, I asked that the whole condo complex be filled with it."

The condo complex must have received it, and apparently the man did, too, because the next day as she arose, she noticed that the front yard had been cleared up. All the trash was gone, and the neighbor actually communicated to her in a friendlier and saner manner than he ever had before. Thankfully, the day after that, the embarrassed owner came home to find some things broken in his house, and was able to get away from his "friend" just long enough to call the police, who finally hauled the man away and ordered him out of town.

This left Christine with one week of peace before she would have to move again, as her temporary sublet was coming to an end. Christine trusted that her next right place would make itself known even though she hadn't yet found it. Having heard about two women who were trying to sell their house, she contacted the ladies and asked about the possibility of staying there for a month while she continued her search for a more permanent residence. The women liked Christine, but didn't know whether their home was sold or not, as they were in the process of negotiating with an interested buyer. Two days before her sublet was to end they told her that if it wasn't sold, she could stay.

The first of the month finally arrived and Christine had to move, however, the women told her they wouldn't have an answer for her until six o'clock that evening. Fifty plants sat in her living room, as well as a truck full of household items that needed to be moved. Pacing back and forth, she observed her process. "I'm noticing I'm stressing. I'm noticing I'm pacing." She asked herself, "Is this healthy?" "No," came the reply.

Rather than continue to pace back and forth, she decided to go for a swim to calm down what she terms, her 'animal body.' Immersing herself in a nearby lake, she felt an overwhelming sense of oneness with the water and the elements. A feeling of bliss enveloped her. Arriving back at the sublet later on, she thought to herself, "I don't have to worry about anything, because everything is appropriate that will come, and I'm here to meet it. The bliss is with me. God is with me."

The women didn't call back until 9:00 p.m. that evening. Although they hadn't heard from their prospective buyer, they told Christine that she could have the house for a month, guaranteed, no matter what.

As Christine's journey unfolds, she continues to create any number of eleventh hour miracles. When things come down to the wire, she says, "I do not want to get in the way of what needs to happen for the Greater Good, so I just keep praying, 'What is the Greater Good here for all beings concerned?' My experience is all about surrendering in faith and trust, and knowing that no matter what happens, it is the appropriate thing to be happening for me in the moment."

Miracle Thinking Tips

- ❧ As a Miracle Thinker, Christine acknowledges that "we live in a soup, in an ocean, of all the goodness in the world. The truth of our being is that everything

– the joy, the support, the awareness, the health, the clarity, the love – is present all the time and in every moment. The reason we don't experience all of this goodness flowing to us is because we've been holding ourselves in an untruth (meaning fear, negativity, lack, or anything else that makes our energy inwardly contract); we restrict wonderful things from flowing to us."

❧ The way to access this abundance? "Relax the untruth," says Christine. Miracle Thinkers must trust, relax and surrender. "When we finally relax our untruth, the abundance just flows. It's like having a cramped leg that gets to stretch. It can hurt at first, but then you get the power of the flow back. When you trust, relax, and surrender, true peace, joy and happiness will rush through you. When we let go of the untruth, we relax into the fullness of our being. Then we realize that God cannot be limited, therefore our experience need not be limited. It often takes time and work to relax out of the untruth. Sometimes you need to take the chisel of awareness and just chip away a little at a time. It's all about trust and surrender."

❧ How did Christine know that she would be safe around the raucous neighbor that night? "I chose to see the truth, so I became still inside," she says. "I quieted my mind, released all fear, and let myself know the truth. We always live in knowingness. You can know just about anything if you quiet the noise or static in your mind. Release the fear, doubt, worry, and any cultural "shoulds." Release any projections that the situation you are in now will unfold just as it has in the past. Then the truth can appear effortlessly in your mind, since you are part of God or universal intelligence."

"Comparing yourself to others is like putting on an emergency brake that will stop you from moving forward in your life."

– Helena Hennessey

The Eyes Have It

In 1985, Helena Hennessey was eating out of trashcans and living under a bridge in Oklahoma City. Addicted to drugs and alcohol, she had been thrown out of a car with two brown sacks of clothes, a half pack of Marlboro Reds, and $1.50 in her pocket by a lover who had had enough.

Helena had never had it easy. At three, she had been left alone in an apartment with two other young siblings for a few weeks while her mother was off shooting heroin. When the Social Services department stepped in, she was placed in foster care, where she was sexually abused by her foster father for years. By age ten, she was drinking, drugging, banging around with gangs, and getting into fights.

Considering that she was living under a bridge, Helena decided that this might be a good time to go to an AA meeting. At her first meeting, she met Sharon, a general contractor twenty years her senior, who she describes as "an angel who God put in my path."

117

Sharon laid down the law, "If you want to start over, you can have my couch and figure out what you want to do. But you can't drink or use drugs, or you'll be out on the street again."

Sharon put Helena to work, paying her $5 an hour to knock out staircases. Swinging a sledgehammer turned out to be 'the best release in the world' for Helena's built up rage. She also began to lift weights. "Being a sexual abuse survivor, I hated my body," she says, "but I wanted control over it. Lifting accomplished that for me."

For a year, Helena slept on Sharon's couch and got clean and sober. One day, however, she stole $600 worth of clothes from a store, justifying her actions to herself by concluding that she couldn't buy clothes on her $5 an hour salary. Later that day, when Sharon knocked on her door saying, "Helena, we need to talk," Helena blew up.

"It was like a 14 year old adolescent snapped off inside of me," says Helena. I was like a street kid again because she was confronting me about my behavior."

Eventually calming down, Helena went to Sharon's room to apologize, and as she did so, a miracle happened. Sharon looked deeply into her eyes and said, "Helena, there is nothing that you will ever do or ever say that will make me stop loving you."

This was the first time Helena had ever experienced unconditional love. Says Helena, "The weirdest thing about it is that they weren't Sharon's eyes. They were God's eyes. That's what I saw. That's what I felt. It was so powerful for me. It was like God jumped into Sharon's body and gave me that message through her. It was the first time in my life I felt like I was really loved or that I existed to be loved."

From that moment on, Helena's life became a succession of wins. She completed vocational rehabilitation, enrolled in college and obtained her degree in Social Work. For two years, she counseled adolescent sexual abuse victims and offenders in a residential sex offender program.

"Working with sex offenders was an incredible part of my healing," says Helena. "Every survivor wonders if they could have done something to make it stop or never happen. When I worked with sex offenders, it became clear to me that they had started grooming the children two years before they had any sexual contact." This gave Helena the validation she needed to understand that it was never her fault.

A few years later, Helena desired to create something new in her life. Moved by Marianne Williamson, who talked about a world where everybody hugged, where everyone's needs were provided for, and where gratitude was key, she decided to create such an environment in the form of a coffeehouse. Shortly thereafter, she found a small storefront to rent. "I wanted to create my own world," says Helena, "and if that world was going to be within 1400 square feet of space, I was going to do it, and that's how big it would be."

She pulled tables out of dumpsters, decoupaged the pressed molding with colorful napkins, and bought an Expresso machine for her new shop, which she named, "Diversity." Customers began piling in, including many who were getting clean and sober. As word about the coffeehouse spread, customers brought in plants, their favorite chairs, or whatever else might be needed. Helena starting holding impromptu events at the shop, and often had a large crowd gathered around her as she worked on mosaic tiling or other art projects.

At one point, Helena noticed certain people frequenting the coffeehouse that she wasn't quite sure about. They were transgendered people in various stages of changing from male to female. When a friend suggested she sit down with 'Cait' and start a conversation over coffee, Helena discovered that Cait was a real person, with real feelings and needs just like anybody else. The two developed a friendship.

"That place saved people's lives," says Helena. "There wasn't a person who came into that place whose name we didn't know. They got a hug. They got a smile. They got conversation."

Since the coffeehouse turned out to be more of a community service than a moneymaker, Helena supported herself by working as a personal trainer. She entered a body building competition and won trophies, as did each of the people she trained. Most importantly, as she strengthened on the outside, she was also strengthening on the inside.

Then, after ten years without contact, Helena learned that her foster father had prostate cancer. "I think the universe has its own justice and that was part of his," says Helena matter-of-factly. She believes that illnesses that happen in specific areas of the body relate to where one is not forgiving of themselves and that "cancer is your body eating your own body through guilt."

She called her foster father, who apologized and took 100 percent accountability for his actions. "I was past the point of wanting his apology or needing it, and I got it," says Helena. "It was a gift. He told me there was nothing I'd done to be a part of that and admitted he was sick. He also told me that he prays for my happiness every day, and that he knows he'll have to make his peace with his Maker."

Helena attributes many of her positive traits to her foster father, from having a work ethic, to saving money, to being dependent on one's self and interdependent with others. "When I first began to recognize those traits of his as being positive in my life, I knew that I was beginning to heal," says Helena.

After running the coffeehouse for five years, Helena decided to pursue her artistic passion full time, sandblasting glass blocks and turning them into candles with swirls of bright airbrushed colors. She also started working in metal, creating customized iron gates embedded with fused glass. Today, she travels the country with her partner, selling her unique objects de 'art. Just as Helena's candles glow, so does Helena, whose bright spirit touches the lives of all she encounters.

In reflection, Helena says, "I started my life as a victim of circumstances. Then I become part of the solution for other victims. That was a full circle for me and it was very healing." She further acknowledges that "there's never been a dream that I've put out there for myself that I've not accomplished. Through the grace of God and some very special people in my life – and being strong-headed, willing and disciplined – I've accomplished all of this. I'm proud of that."

Miracle Thinking Tips

- Helena observes that many people compare their lives to hers, and invalidate their own pain as a result. Miracle Thinkers must avoid comparing themselves to others because "comparing oneself to another is like putting on an emergency brake that will stop you from moving forward in your life." Says Helena, "I have learned that everybody has their own journey. Their pain is different than mine, but no more or less intense than my pain was to me."

✦ If you want to be a Miracle Thinker, "start by loving yourself," says Helena. "There are so many desperate people in this world wanting to be loved. The truth is that when you love yourself, you have more love than you know what to do with in a lifetime, and then you start giving it out. It's only when we don't have it that we're selfish, and we want to hold onto it and get it from other people."

✦ Helena says she's always wanted a bubble machine because "who can walk by a bubble machine and not smile?" In spite of every adversity they've endured, Miracle Thinkers often have a deep down desire to be lighthearted and uplift others. "I've run across my story a million times and worse," says Helena. "What makes me still have the capacity to love, to believe, to have faith? The miracle in my life is that I love life. I believe more in the hope of mankind than not."

"When you ask for miracles to flow through you to others, it will be a joy to get up every morning wondering what miracles the day will bring."

– Mary Ellen Angelscribe

For Remembering to Follow Your Intuition . . .

A Final Goodbye

While working in a Canadian health food store, Mary Ellen met Della, a young woman of the Cowichan's First Nation tribe. When Mary Ellen asked Della if she had any stinging nettle, which was an herb used for healing that she could plant in her yard, Della laughed, saying, "Stinging nettle is a nasty weed that people try to get rid of, not plant." The two quickly become friends.

One night, Mary Ellen dreamt that Della phoned her. Since Della didn't have a phone or car, Mary Ellen drove to her home in the morning to check up on her as the dream had a disturbing sense of urgency to it.

Della was, indeed, very upset. The minister of her church, a young man in his late thirties, had suddenly fallen into an unexplained life-threatening coma. Della didn't know what she could do, only that she wanted to do something. However, she had no way of getting to the hospital. When Mary Ellen appeared out of the blue, Della knew it was a sign that they were meant to help the minister in some way.

The two arrived at the hospital, still not knowing exactly why they were there or what they would do. Seventy First Nations people lined the corridor, all waiting in silence, while others surrounded the bedside of the dying man.

Running her fingers over the minister's head, Della located a large lump. She showed a respected Native healer how to do a manipulation, while the others in the room prayed in their many languages.

Having taken a weekend course in foot reflexology, Mary Ellen had learned that the nerves in the big toe were directly connected to the brain. Since the dying man was in a coma, she decided to forcefully poke the brain point on his big toe three times.

All of a sudden, the dying man bolted upright, yelling "STOP! STOP! STOP!" in his Native tongue. As a swarm of people rushed in upon hearing the voice of their beloved preacher, Mary Ellen quietly exited.

The minister remained fully alert through the day and late into the night. He was able to tell his son how much he loved him and apologize to him for not being there for him. He was also able to tell his wife how much he loved her. Then, the following morning, he died.

Miracle Thinking Tips

- Miracle Thinkers follow through when they receive intuitive messages – even if the reason for their intuitive urge has no apparent explanation. As a Miracle Thinker, not only did Mary Ellen develop the receptivity to receive a message through her dreams, but she chose to act on that intuition even though she had no idea what the message meant; she drove to Della's, trusting that there was a purpose in having received that message. As a result, a young man was able to say a final farewell to his loved ones.

- Mary Ellen encourages Miracle Thinkers to consciously make the choice to be a vehicle for God. "Ask in your heart for miracles to flow through you into the lives of others." When you make that choice, she says, "It's a joy to get up every morning wondering what miracle the day is going to bring."

- Miracle Thinkers know that everything they've learned contributes to the Highest Good of the present moment. Just as a weekend course in reflexology miraculously enabled a man to temporarily "leap" out of a coma, so too, do we all have gifts that can benefit others. Miracle Thinkers believe they have something to give. Because they feel like they have something worth sharing, great gifts of knowledge are often bestowed upon them.

"Our miracles don't just come through the hand of God, they come through the hands of people. We are here to be each other's angels."

– Randy Peyser

For Manifesting Things You Want . . .

The Gift

(Author Story)

From the time I was six-years-old, I was passionate about playing drums. However, the closest I ever got to trying one was to play my kneecaps with my hands. Even in my teens, though, I still fantasized about being a drummer.

Years later, I happened to pick up a music catalog. A bright red drum set caught my eye and just about leapt off the page. It made me so happy that I cut out the picture and taped it to a filing cabinet where I could see it from my desk at the senior center where I worked.

One morning, I heard a flurry of beautiful music coming from the center's dining room. Upon investigation, I discovered an elderly woman sitting at the piano bench, expertly playing away. A few days later, a new gentleman arrived at the center. He was a retired clarinet player. Within a short time of having introduced the musicians to one another, a band was formed. The pianist's husband played the electric bass guitar, and a drummer one of them knew rounded out the ensemble.

Every Tuesday, the newly formed group played their toe-tapping Dixieland jazz for the center's tea dances. In fact, pretty soon, they were playing at all the senior centers in the county. It brought me great joy to stand near the drummer and watch every move he made as he beat the drumheads and crashed the cymbals.

After four years of great music, though, the drummer died. Months later, I happened to meet his wife. She thanked me for the joy I'd brought to her husband through the band I'd helped create. In the course of our conversation, I asked her if she intended to sell the drums. She wanted to, however, her husband had told her not to get less than $3000 for them, which was way out of my league.

A year passed by. Then, out of the blue, the woman called. The drums had been sitting in a storage shed, and she wanted to give them to someone who would really appreciate them and use them. Within a half hour, a $3000 drum set sat in my living room and a lifelong dream was fulfilled.

Miracle Thinking Tips

* The things we really want often come in mysterious ways. As Miracle Thinkers, we don't have to know how these things will find us, only that they are things that we truly desire and support us in our highest good.

- Miracle Thinkers sometimes make treasure maps that include the images of things they want to create in their lives. Even though I didn't consciously realize that the image of the drum set I'd put up on my filing cabinet at work was a treasure map, I believe it certainly helped me to achieve my desired result.

- Miracle Thinkers understand that our miracles don't just come through the hand of God, they come through the hands of people as well. We are here to be each other's angels and help each other achieve our miracles. Because this expensive gift was given freely, I learned that I could pass along expensive items that I no longer needed to help create someone else's miracle, too. Joy goes round in circles. Just as I originally helped the drummer to find great joy in his life, even after his death, he still helped me to find great joy in mine.

"I asked myself, 'Why is she the chosen one?' I heard, 'Because she chose to be chosen.' So I chose to be Number One and my miracles began."

– Terri Amos

How Miss USA Became A-Okay

Springtime in New York seemed like the perfect time for Terri Amos to fly in for her first book tour from her home in Southern California. However, when the new author arrived in the Big Apple, Mother Nature greeted her with a snowstorm, howling winds and freezing cold. The last place the former Miss USA beauty pageant winner wanted to be was outdoors on a day like this. Fortunately, the only pressing matter on her agenda was a radio interview, which could be accomplished from the warmth of her hotel room.

Even so, Terri felt an inner sense of conflict. After all, it was New York and she was only going to be there for ten days. Shouldn't she be doing something or going somewhere? Certainly, it wasn't right to just be sitting around all day long doing nothing. Then the phone rang. It was her manager insisting that she see a particular Broadway show. So Terri jumped on her computer. However, when she saw the price of the tickets, she nearly fell out of her seat.

Dropping the show idea, she decided to do what she had really wanted to do all along, which was to spend the day in her robe, eating whatever she wanted to eat, and basically, "being a slug." Tomorrow she would get up, go to the gym and face the world, but today she would forgo the guilt of not being productive, and just lounge around and "take care of Terri."

Since her hotel didn't have an exercise room, the next morning, she trotted off to a nearby gym. While waiting for a class to begin, she happened to strike up a conversation with a fellow student, and after the class, the two continued to talk. The woman asked Terri if she intended to see any plays while she was in town. Terri mentioned her manager's insistence that she see that certain Broadway show, but how the price of the tickets had put the idea out of the question.

The woman replied, "I work where that show is playing. How about being my guest? I'll take you this week.

A few days later, Terri got to see the Broadway hit from the best seats in the house.

Miracle Thinking Tips

✦ Says Terri, "We send messages to our children that you have to push, push, push to be something in this world. The truth is that if you honor and love yourself, and do what it is that you really want to do – instead of what you think you have to do or should do – then the Universe is going to do the same for you. At first, I believed I had to be out hustling in New York, but as soon as I loved and honored myself by hanging out in my hotel room all day, the very next day, the Universe provided for me."

* "If you want miracles to happen in your life, you must believe you are worthy of miracles," says Terri. "I was Miss USA 1982. I had spent my whole life trying to get attention and be something so that people would love me. Even in that moment of winning Miss USA, I didn't believe that I was really worthy of that kind of miracle, and I felt confused. I didn't realize then that I had a running theme in my life where I always felt like I was second choice. Years later, I had a friend who constantly seemed to have miracles happen to her. "I would ask myself, 'Why is she always the chosen one? Why can't I be the chosen one?' While meditating, I heard, 'Terri, she's chosen because she has chosen to be chosen. She has chosen to be Number One.' In that moment, I said, 'I am choosing to be Number One.' Immediately I started having miracles happen."

* "The universe is a mirror," continues Terri. "It's going to give us whatever we are giving to ourselves. When we know our truth, and stand in it, and do not diverge from it, the Universe says, 'I want to take care of you.' When we finally believe in our heart that we can be Number One, and we love ourselves and treat ourselves as Number One, the Universe says, 'She's treating herself as Number One, so we can treat her that way as well.'"

"Healing can only take place in the peace of the present moment. If you want to heal, you have to get to a place of peace."

– Thomas Day Oates

For Finding Peace Within . . .

The Presence of Peace

Back in the Fall of '89, a twenty-something insurance salesman named Thomas Day Oates Jr. was rapidly working his way toward making a million dollars. Hot on the money trail, the overly-zealous salesman paid little attention to the fact that he was in a constant state of stress. Even when the flu hit him hard, he refused to be knocked down. Instead, he pushed himself even more.

However, this "flu" didn't quit. At first, only his joints ached, but then his hair began to fall out and his weight dropped. In addition, he was consumed by a crushing feeling of fatigue. Finding himself in a continual state of exhaustion, the once active, young man was quickly reduced to the status of an invalid.

For the next four-and-a-half years, Thomas, who was eventually diagnosed with Chronic Fatigue Syndrome, devoted his days to stewing over this illness that had taken his life away from him. However, after months of bitter anger, followed by frustration and bouts of depression, he eventually resigned himself to the conclusion that his health might never return.

So, he let go of his future dreams of having a family, making the big bucks, or of having any sort of a normal life. With nothing but time on his hands and the bed in which he lay, he thought about the people who had made up his life until now. He recalled painful past events and sought to forgive anyone who had ever hurt him and forgave himself. He let go of any regrets he had about his past. Finally, he surrendered the need for his life to be any other way than the way it was. Now there was nothing left to do, but be. For days at a time, he experienced complete stillness and quiet.

From this still and resigned place, he watched the light on the trees change as Spring turned to Summer, and Summer turned to Fall. The light falling on the trees and the changing of the colors captivated his attention and moved him into the present moment. Then a strange thing started to occur: Thomas felt himself filled with a sense of deep, infinite peace, joy and grace. This feeling of peace was so strong that, in every moment, he found himself feeling present, calm, and accepting of whatever was. He says, "It was truly heaven on earth."

As he embraced the stillness and this newfound sense of peace, a joyful knowing began to take hold and his life purpose began to percolate. Somehow he knew without a doubt that he was going to heal. He didn't know how or when, and truthfully, by this point he didn't even care. All he knew was that he felt so joyful in this state of grace and peace that it no longer mattered to him if his body got well.

Rather than continue to dwell on the person he could no longer be or what he could no longer do, he decided to put his fifteen minutes worth of good energy per day into something he could do. Since he'd always enjoyed taking pictures, he chose to walk around his yard and photograph whatever beauty he discovered. In time, he noticed that the more he focused on this joyful activity, the more his energy appeared to be returning.

A year-and-a-half later, he felt well enough to take a few photography classes. In time, he journeyed to Portland, Oregon, where he was awed by the beauty of the rugged coastline of the Northwest. He decided to take film classes. Video camera in hand, he began shooting the most captivating light and the most beautiful places along the Oregon-California coast he could find. It was his hope that by viewing such stunning natural beauty, others who were ill could be drawn into the present moment in a powerfully, beautiful way and experience the kind of peace that he had found. He especially wanted to help those who were lying in hospital beds, since hospitals are breeding grounds for anxiety and fear.

His films incorporated music by Native American flautist, R. Carlos Nakai, along with scenes of the ocean at dawn and sunset. His second video, which won an International Health and Medical Media Award known as, "The Freddie Award," is now in use in over 750 hospitals and health care institutions around the country, including the Mayo Clinic and St. Jude Children's Research Hospital. His video is also being used by the U.S. Navy, by stock-traders, and by other individuals who find themselves in frequent, heightened states of anxiety.

Miracle Thinking Tips

✦ "Healing can only take place in the peace of the present moment. If you want to heal, you have to get to a place of peace. You can't heal if you are fearful, angry, frustrated or terrified, because emotions such as fear, anger, and regret are rooted in the past or future, and will pull you away from the peace of the Now."

✦ "Healing doesn't necessarily mean your body recovers. Rather, healing is moving towards peace. Let go of the barriers (fear, wants, regrets and past hates) that keep you from seeing and being the peace that is all around you. Whether you are looking for health, wealth, a mate, or whatever, the anxious stewing over a goal not met will keep you from being present, and therefore, separated from the healing peace and love that we swim in at all times."

✦ If you want to experience peace, "pray this one prayer from the bottom of your heart: '*If there is a God, please show me. I want to know . . . Please.*' This simple prayer should come with a warning label, however, because after you offer this prayer, whatever is keeping you from experiencing God's peace in the present moment will systematically be eliminated, regardless of what you think, believe or do. Then, when your life begins to resemble dirt clods that have been hurled against a brick wall, the trick is to not resist the disaster. Let it go. Let go of the people, the friends, the goals, the job, everything. The more quickly you embrace the letting go, the sooner the walls to the present will come down. Then you will fall without effort into a place of unspeakable peace.

"Put your arms out by your sides, palms up, and ask to be led to your highest happiness. Then go for a quiet walk in nature and listen to the Divine from within."

– Randy Peyser

A Chance Encounter

(Author Story)

Having moved to a small town hours away from where I'd been living, I hardly new a soul. Even after a year, I still felt very isolated and alone in the world. One day, when I was feeling particularly lonely, I went to see a therapist. At the end of our session, he delivered a very strange message: "I don't know why I'm telling you this, but there is a massage school just a few minutes from here that you might want to know about."

Being open to his flash of psychic receptivity, I thought that perhaps there might be someone for me to meet at that school, or a note on a bulletin board that I might need to see. Who knew? Feeling the slightest glimmer of possibility, I sped off to the school.

The only person on the premises was the Registrar. We had a little chat, but no bells went off. Next, I perused the announcements on their bulletin board. Nothing caught my eye. "Oh well," I thought, giving up on the idea that anything out of the ordinary might happen.

Since the ocean was just an arm's throw away, I decided I might as well go for a walk on the beach. The fog was thick and the air was nippy, so after a brisk walk, I quickly headed back to my car.

By now, it was way past lunchtime and my stomach was growling. Even though there was a nice looking Mexican restaurant right in front of me as I waited for a red light to turn green, I decided I'd better wait until I got home. That way I could save a few dollars, even though it would take me about an hour to arrive at my front door. All of a sudden, I changed my mind. "No! I'm hungry now," I thought. "I can treat myself to lunch."

Except for the cashier, the large restaurant was empty. However, as I placed my order, a woman entered. Since we were the only two people in the entire restaurant, I asked her if she'd like to have some company over lunch. She hesitated, then decided to take me up on my offer. As we pulled back a couple of chairs, I introduced myself.

"I know you!" she exclaimed. It turned out that eight years ago, I had interviewed this woman for an article I was writing for a magazine. At the time, she'd lived four hours north of where we were currently sitting. She'd moved to my area only recently to assist her mother during an illness. Now that her mother had passed, she was feeling lost in her life and unsure of her direction.

As we ate our lunches and talked up a storm, both of us felt uplifted. Here we were – two souls who had been brought together after having met only once eight years previously in a town many hours away. Both of us had been feeling disconnected and alone, as well as unsure of our paths in life. What were the odds that the two of us would meet at that particular restaurant at that particular moment?

Miracle Thinking Tips

✦ We are never alone – even when we mistakenly might think we are. We are always connected to something greater than ourselves. If you are feeling truly desperate, ask for help. Ask to be given a sign that you are not alone. Put your arms out by your sides, palms up, and ask to be led to your highest happiness. Then go for a quiet walk in nature and listen to the Divine from within.

✦ Take notice of any synchronicities that show up in your life. Messages and guidance from above will come your way. All you have to do is notice it when it does.

✦ If you don't put yourself first, then why should the Universe put you first? Miracle Thinkers understand the importance of nurturing themselves. The wonderfully synchronistic moment in this story happened immediately after I made the decision to take care of myself and eat right at that moment, instead of waiting another hour. All it took was the simple willingness to nurture myself for that magical encounter to then unfold.

"Say 'yes' to unexpected opportunities. A 'yes' can open more doors than you can ever imagine."

– Randy Peyser

For Opening to Your Highest Good...

Just Say 'Yes'

(Author Story)

During a magazine interview I was conducting, author, Wayne Dyer, once told me that he never declines an offer to be interviewed by anybody in the media because of the following experience: As one of America's most inspirational authors, he had been traveling coast to coast on a book talk circuit, but he was less than thrilled about the prospect of doing one particular radio show because, besides being exhausted, this station wasn't even very popular. However, he had agreed to do the interview and he intended to keep his word. So, he dragged himself into the studio.

At the end of the interview, the phone rang and a caller said, "I was sitting in a baseball stadium trying to tune into the game on my radio, and as I turned the dial, I heard you speaking, so I listened. I was feeling really suicidal. After what you said, I don't want to kill myself anymore. I just want to thank you for being there and saying what you did."

Just by showing up, Wayne had helped save someone's life. At that moment, he realized that each opportunity to appear on a show or be interviewed was actually a call from God to serve.

Miracle Thinking Tips

- Miracle Thinkers say "yes" to life. A "yes" can open more doors than you can ever imagine. Miracle Thinkers also say "yes" to unexpected opportunities. A friend, named Ben, who works in a helping profession, wanted to expand his business. One day, he received a phone call from a producer at a major radio station who had seen his ad in a local magazine. He was invited to be a guest on their show, but turned the opportunity down because the station focused on hip-hop music. Ben didn't perceive the listeners of hip hop as the music as the kind of people who would solicit his services. Three months later, he was struggling to make ends meet, wondering how to make money and get the word out about his work. What might have happened if he had said, "yes," to that opportunity?

- One of the biggest keys to creating miracles involves your willingness to receive whatever good comes your way – in whatever form it shows up. In order to achieve a miracle you must be open to it. You must feel worthy of receiving, without making up a story as to why you should not receive something at this moment, or why you should turn down an opportunity. If you deny the tiny examples of good that come your way, you'll block an even greater flow of miracles. To strengthen your receiving muscle, say, "yes," to all the little miracles, those positive things, that are offered to you.

* Miracle Thinkers speak up! You never know who might be touched by your words or who needs to hear what you have to say. Everyone has wisdom to share. Your voice counts.

"If you think you have a money problem, what you really have is a receiving problem. Be willing to receive whatever good comes your way."

– Gary Douglas

The Quickest Way to a Million Dollar Mindset

(Author Story)

It started with my big toe. Racing off to a business meeting, I'd squeezed my feet into a tight pair of heels. A month later, when the pain in my toe still hadn't gone away, I decided to see a podiatrist, and eventually, an MRI was arranged.

I'd never had an MRI before. All I knew about them was that they were noisy. That was an understatement. Being a sensitive kind of gal, the constant clanging and banging and weird sounds made me want to run away screaming. Of course, I wasn't going anywhere while lying on a slab with my foot wedged in gigantic wads of foam.

After the first twenty minutes, I surrendered in disgust to the idea that I'd just have to endure this horrendous racket for as long as it lasted. Then another idea occurred to me: What if every single sound that was blasting my eardrums represented some form of money coming to me?

In the background I could hear, 'wee-hoo, wee-hoo, wee-hoo.'

I imagined that every 'wee-hoo' was a slab of thousand dollar bills being pressed for me. Then there were the fast clinks. Those were the nickel slots. The clinks got deeper. Those were my quarters coming down the shoot from the quarter slots. Then faster and with more bass . . . my Susan B. Anthony silver dollars. Then the really loud hoof beats. Of course! It was a bull market and all those funds and investments were coming my way! Then the 'chok chok choks' . . . my rows of houses being built. Hundreds of patinks . . . my bags and bags of diamonds. 'Snup snup snup' . . . My bonds being printed. 'Swip, swip swip' . . . my hundred dollar bills. 'Sshloop, sshloop, sshloop' . . . my bars of gold. 'Dankety doinkety dink' . . . my rows of corn . . . my commodities! Meanwhile, the 'wee-hoo's continued in the background, which meant there was no end to the $1000 dollar bills still coming my way.

As long as a particular sound continued, I stayed open to receive that form of abundance. As a result, I pushed way beyond any internal limits I had ever consciously or subconsciously set for myself as to how much I could receive.

As I left the MRI, I was wearing a million dollar smile. I felt happy and exhilarated. Then about an hour-and-a-half later, the MRI department called. "We had a problem with our equipment and we need to do it all over again."

By the time I emerged from the second MRI, I was a millionaire a zillion times over. If there was any invisible barrier left that had separated me from wealth – from this lifetime or any other – I was sure I had broken through it.

Within days, my income began to reflect my new perception. My phone started ringing off the wall with clients eager for my book publishing services, and more new doors opened. In fact, those doors have never closed. They just continue to keep on opening to even greater degrees with every clink, chok, snup, swip, shloop, and dankety-doinkety-dink I think of. Wee-hoo!

Miracle Thinking Tips

- Gary Douglas, a facilitator of transformation, (www.accessraz.com), believes that nobody has a money problem. Instead, he says, "If you think you have a money problem, what you really have is a receiving problem." The key, then, is to increase your capacity to receive more, which can be accomplished in numerous ways – besides by having an MRI.

- Miracles come to those with high self-esteem. Children who are loved have higher self-esteem than those who aren't. They find it easier to accept the good being offered them, because they automatically feel deserving of it. Children who are not loved are accustomed to not receiving, and are also more likely to deny love or reject other good things when they are offered. How can anyone who was mistreated at an early age feel deserving when they were always told they weren't enough? If you were "not enough" as a child, how can you be "enough" to receive something as great as a miracle now? While you can't change your childhood, you can raise your self-esteem and your ability to receive by showing the Universe that you value yourself.

- To value yourself, speak up and set boundaries with others so that your needs are made known . Instead of always giving to others, put yourself first for once. In fact, put yourself first a lot. If you think you are being selfish, don't worry. Typically, the ones who are being selfish are the ones who don't have a clue that they're being selfish. If it's on your conscience, you are most likely not being selfish, but are in the early stages of learning what it feels like to put yourself and your needs first.

- What do you want to see multiply in your personal world? Start giving yourself what you want to receive. For example, I wanted to receive more money, so I started giving myself more money through the MRI visualization.

"Behind all hatred lies a deep desire to be loved. Strive to bring difficult interactions back to a place of love."

– Joe Westerhaver

Love Has No Opposite

Did you ever have a person come into your life for no longer than the blink of an eye, who left an indelible impression on you just the same? A retired Air Force pilot, named Joe Westerhaver, was one such person in my life. One day, while in the midst of an inspiring conversation, this amazing man declared to me that "love has no opposite." "What about hate? What about fear?" I asked, believing that these were two likely candidates. Joe responded by sharing the following miracle story:

"When my son Jim was in his mid-thirties, he was once again diagnosed with an aggressive form of Non-Hodgkins Lymphoma. The chemotherapy scheduled for treating this particular occurrence was to be far more damaging and life-threatening than had been the case the first time the cancer had occurred. One day, when it looked like the end was drawing near, we were driving down a freeway. My son was at the wheel. Wondering if there was anything left unsaid between us, I asked, "If there's anything you want to tell me, what would it be?"

He paused, then slowly and deliberately formed the words, "I - hate - you."

What followed were a barrage of "I hate you's" in which my son screamed and swore up a storm as he expressed his resentment towards me for being an absentee father. It was true. Due to my Air Force career, and all the other ways in which I had never shown up for him in his life, I had been an absentee father. He was so full of rage, he reached over and started punching me. At this point, the car was weaving all over the freeway, while I was being backhanded at 80 miles an hour."

Startled, I asked Joe, "Well, what did you do?"

"I took it," said Joe, calmly and with much compassion in his voice. "You see, I knew that he couldn't have hated me that much if he didn't love me that much."

The bottom line is that Joe's son's life-threatening condition went into a rare form of regression, which did not require additional treatment. Although they had their ups and downs, father and son enjoyed having a closer relationship filled with love and respect for one another for ten more years, until the son's eventual passing.

Miracle Thinking Tips

- ✦ Miracle Thinkers look for the Love that powers all interactions. Sometimes a Miracle Thinker has to peek under every nook and cranny to find the love or the good in a difficult situation. But with determination, it can be found.

* Miracle Thinkers acknowledge that Love is the ultimate goal. They know that behind all hatred and anger, people have a deep desire to be loved. Therefore, Miracle Thinkers strive to bring difficult interactions back to a place of love.

* A Miracle Thinker would never dismiss another's pain as being trivial. When pain is being expressed by another, Miracle Thinkers listen deeply without judging. By acknowledging an expression of pain in this manner, Miracle Thinkers realize that they are setting the stage for the emotional pain to possibly be moved out of the sufferer's body.

"The universe will co-create with you, but just as you had to do your own homework in 5th grade instead of your parents, the Universe encourages your active participation."

– Randy Peyser

For Manifesting the Perfect House . . .

Time Never Runs Out

When their old, rented, 1300 square foot cracker box could no longer hold Elissa Rigzin Giles, her husband, two teenagers and an eight-year-old, the couple decided to buy a slightly larger place nearby. However, within three years, Elissa realized that she needed to be living in a larger country setting.

Her husband initially agreed with her, but would not agree to put their house on the market until their new home was a certainty. After some searching, they found a Christmas tree farm, which contained a fairly new house that appealed to the husband. Situated near a creek, the location felt very remote, but was only 40 minutes away from a buzzing city.

Unfortunately, the asking price for the farm was $150,000 more than the couple could reasonably spend. But since they really wanted it, they put their current house on the market for an extremely high price, hoping to create more money to put towards the down payment they would need.

Watching their home sit on the market for months, their Realtor pleaded with them to lower their price. Meanwhile, the farm was still available, although the couple worried that someone else might buy it. In her gut, though, Elissa felt like they were supposed to live at that new location.

Finally one day, a couple viewed Elissa's home and offered their full asking price. While signing the deal, Elissa happened to notice the couple's former address; it was the same house that Elissa and her husband had moved from previously.

The next day, Elissa and her husband made an offer on the farm. To their amazement, they found out that the owners of the farmhouse had decided to take it off the market the following day because it wasn't selling. Says Elissa: "They were shocked. We were shocked. We made a deal on the very last day of the listing."

Miracle Thinking Tips

✦ Time never runs out; it is always possible for your miracle to happen. When there is something that is meant for your Highest Good, it will arrive – it's just a matter of "when." Allow your sense of trust to expand because that which is right for you will ultimately be there. You can strengthen your ability to trust by understanding that miracles respond to patience and divine right timing.

✦ To know if your desired goal is in your highest and best interest, pay attention to your feelings. Highest and best goals are the ones that bring up your passion and energize you. They are the ones that make you lighten up when you talk about them. If you feel a special feeling in your gut or heart, your goal is spot on.

* The universe loves to co-create with you, but just as you had to do your own homework in fifth grade and not have a parent do it for you, the Universe encourages your active participation. While miracles respond to patience and divine right timing, you must take action steps and follow through in order to create your desired results. Action steps can range from praying to picking up the phone. You know what you need to do. Become the "pitbull of perseverance" and just do it!

"All prayers are heading to the same Source, regardless of the beliefs of the person praying. In other words, 'Same God— different wrapper."

– Randy Peyser

For Finding Lost Objects ...

When The Saints Come Marching In

(Author Story)

Even though the old gold watch didn't work anymore, I rarely took it off my wrist. Forty years ago, my mother had given this delicate little timepiece to her mother. Eventually, my grandmother had passed it down to me.

One day when the watch turned up missing, I tore the house apart looking for it, but I couldn't find it anywhere. Although it wasn't worth much, its sentimental value was priceless. I was distraught. It couldn't have fallen off my hand. The elastic gold chain strap was fine, and even if it had broken, I was pretty sure I would have heard it fall. I tried desperately to think if I had taken it off or where I might have put it. After two or three months went by, I resigned myself to the fact that it was gone forever.

One evening, I went to out dinner with a friend and during our conversation, I happened to mention the missing watch to her. She offered to state a prayer for its safe return. I thought, why not? So we moved our dinner plates to the side, and she held my hands in the middle of the restaurant and closed her eyes and said a prayer. She told me that St. Anthony was the finder of lost objects, and she asked St. Anthony to bring this beloved object back to me quickly and safely. The prayer complete, we went back to our dinner and the conversation moved on.

A day or two later, I noticed that my car was streaked with grime. When was the last time I'd washed it anyway? I couldn't even remember. So I grabbed the plastic bucket filled with some squeegies, soap, and my big yellow rubber gloves and headed outside. But when I tried to pull on the gloves, I couldn't; there was something inside one of them. Of course, it was my grandmother's watch. Obviously, the friction from the thick rubber gloves had pulled the chain link band off my hand the last time I'd washed the car. I didn't think I'd ever see that watch again. And here it was, safe and sound all along, just waiting for me to find it.

Miracle Thinking Tips

    ✦ A TV host once looked at me rather puzzled and said: "You were born Jewish, your books are spiritually eclectic, and you speak in churches. How do you account for all of this? What immediately came out of my mouth in response was: "Same God, different wrapper." Miracle Thinkers understand that all prayers are heading to the same God, regardless of the background of the person who is praying. My friend was calling on a saint for help. Even though I was not Christian, by realizing that we all come from the same Source, I accepted her prayers. By staying open and being receptive, this miracle occurred.

❋ A dear friend and mentor, Reverend Delorise Lucas, always said, "Pray to whomever you love. You can pray to Jesus, or God, or Buddha, or whomever you want. The only thing that matters is that you love them."

❋ After you've prayed for whatever it is you want to find – whether it be a missing object or anything you've been searching for in your life – let it go. In the example above, after my friend and I had prayed, we quickly changed subjects and didn't give the matter a second thought. By doing so, we allowed the universe to do its magic, and the miracle unfolded quickly, much to my surprise and delight.

"For important communications, ask your Intermediary tions, ask your Intermediary Angel to speak with the other person's Intermediary Angel, and ask that your information easily be understood."

– Reverend Delorise Lucas

Portrait of A Miracle Thinker

(Author Story)

Shortly after his high school graduation, Neil Khanna was injured in a hit-and-run car accident involving a drunk driver. As a result, four disks in Neil's neck and back were ruptured. Over the next four years, Neil suffered from extreme pain, which the specialists eventually said he'd just have to learn to live with.

One day, a friend told Neil's mother about a visiting faith healer named, Reverend Delorise Lucas. Affectionately called, "Momma," the minister traveled around the country, holding classes and performing healings on people and their pets. Feeling an overwhelming urge to meet this lady, Neil insisted that his mother take him to see her.

"I did not know what to expect," says Neil. "Momma explained to everyone what was going to happen and where the power was coming from (God). After working on someone, she turned to me and said, 'You have a pain in your back and have come for a healing.' Watching her work, I was totally amazed at her abilities, and when she asked me to be next, I went to sit in the chair in the middle of the room.

During the healing, the people in the room sang the words, "Praise God," to the tune of "Amazing Grace." I fell into a meditative state, and suddenly, I felt an enormous warmth and surge of energy enter from the top of my head and shoot down my spine. My skin turned completely flush over my entire body and the pain left me; I was instantly healed. I said, 'Thank you,' to Momma, and she replied, "Don't thank me—thank God." That was years ago, and I haven't had a pain since.

Rev. Delorise Lucas of Columbus, Ohio died in September of 2002. Having had ten Near Death Experiences previously, she used to describe death as a joyous reunion with those you love on the other side. She called it, "going to the party." In fact, in the late '90's when a TWA plane exploded midair, she quietly said, "200 people just went to the party."

I (Randy) studied with this most remarkable woman for many years and watched as she prayed and did a laying on of hands for whomever was put in her path. She would explain that healing could happen in an instant. The first time I met Momma, she put her hand on a breast lump I had and within two minutes it was gone. Absolutely startled at the immediate transformation that had just occurred in my body, I asked her, "How did you do that?" In the humble way that she always spoke, she replied, "I just wanted to give you a demonstration of God in action. God doesn't half-step; God whole-steps."

She warned that people could prolong the length of time necessary for their healing, or counteract their healing, through the power of their own thoughts and their degree of disbelief.

To counteract those beliefs, she'd issue the directives: "Doubt get out! Fear get away from here! Send your doubt and fear to the River of Forgetfulness where it forgets to come back!"

If someone was afraid to declare something positive for themselves – for example, "I'm happy," or "things are finally going right for me" – for fear that if they said these statements out loud their opposite would occur, Momma instructed them to add the phrase, "through the Grace of God," to their original statement.

Momma never charged for her services, although donations were heartily accepted to support the house full of children she adopted. I never saw her keep anything for herself.

From early morning until late at night, she worked with people who were enduring the most difficult of circumstances, yet she was the happiest person I've ever met. One of her best pieces of advice to me: "Don't let nothing or nobody steal your joy."

Miracle Thinking Tips

- As a Miracle Thinker, Momma saw the beauty in all people and had an uncanny way of bringing out the best in each one. She taught about loving without conditions. In her words, "If you can learn to love without a condition, you will see all the beautiful people. Some people have conditions that they love you 'because' . . . If you can just love, and love that person's soul and spirit, then all you see is the beauty in them. And that's all you need to see – all the good that can come from them. I guess that's what I was blessed to see."

✦ Miracle Thinkers seek the Highest Good for all. Momma prayed for the greatest good to unfold for each person, no matter who they were. If someone came to her because they were having problems with an argumentative or spiteful person, in addition to praying for the person seeking help, she'd ask God to bring the difficult person to his next highest elevation. If you are having problems with a difficult person, ask in prayer that he be brought to his next highest elevation.

✦ Here is another powerful method from Momma that allows communication to flow more smoothly between two beings: She would say that every person has an Intermediary Angel. When you want to communicate something important – such as to a spouse, your boss, or your pet – first, ask your Intermediary Angel to speak with that other being's Intermediary Angel, and ask that the information you share with the other be more easily integrated and understood. If a battle is in progress between you and another, call on Archangel Michael to cut through any communication barriers with his mighty sword.

"Visualize exactly what it is you want. Then remember that how it comes together is not up to you; it's up to the heavenly 'Ways and Means Committee.'"

– Ronnie Chittum

The Power of A Bubble *or* When To Play with Fire

When the largest fire in the United States consumed 500,000 acres in southern Oregon, Ronnie Chittum quickly discovered the impact of prayer and visualization firsthand. Having been given 45 minutes notice to vacate her property along 20 acres on the Illinois River, Ronnie imagined a bubble of light surrounding her home and adjoining twin cabins. She envisioned what she calls "the Universal Light of God" protecting the sanctuary that had been her dream home since childhood. Around the same time, two neighbors appeared and attached hoses to the top of the three buildings. Then they all fled before the fire consumed the area.

No one knows for sure how long the water dripped down the roof before the water tank dried up and the hoses melted. However, when Ronnie was able to return to the completely burnt grounds, she discovered that her home and the two cabins remained untouched.

Endeavoring to see all of the good that could come from such an experience, Ronnie observed that even though she had lost 50 percent of the fir and oak trees on her property, when the rainy season eventually came, as much as one hundred new oak shoots were sprouting up from the bases of her badly burnt trees, sprinklings of wild flowers and sweet peas that hadn't been seen in twenty years graced her grounds, and numerous types of birds that hadn't been spotted before appeared.

Interestingly, three years prior to the blaze – and much to the disapproval and warnings of everyone with whom she had consulted – she had created a pond. As it turned out, however, during this out-of-control inferno, the forest service was able to pump out every drop of water in the pond to help bring the fire under control. 5000 gallons of water in the middle of a forest was certainly a miracle in their eyes.

Miracle Thinking Tips

* Miracle Thinkers believe that something good will ultimately come out of a disastrous experience, even if they are not yet sure what that positive outcome is. Since they believe that everything happens for a reason, they know that the disastrous events in their lives don't just occur randomly for the sake of throwing them off-kilter. Instead, they believe that a greater purpose is being served; perhaps they will learn something, develop greater compassion for others, or their lives will unfold in a new way.

* Miracle Thinkers use the powers of prayer and visualization to create what they want. When they are

in any sort of perceived trouble, they are quick to visualize a white or gold light for protection, while invoking the name of a Higher Source.

❋ As a Miracle Thinker, Ronnie Chittum knew that "what you concentrate on is what you get." Therefore, she realized that if she created fearful pictures in her mind, she would experience a fearful outcome. Even though she was overwhelmed by the magnitude of the fire, she made a powerful decision to focus only on the result she wanted. Ronnie says, "If you want to be a Miracle Thinker, visualize exactly what it is you want. Then remember that how it comes together is not up to you; it's up to the heavenly 'Ways and Means Committee.'"

"Never forget that love is all that counts. Always"

– Voice from the other side, speaking
to Nadia McCaffrey in a coma

The Little Mother in the Sky

What better way to spend a summer afternoon in the French countryside than picking fragrant sweet pea flowers in the wheat field next to Grandma's house? Unfortunately, seven year old, Nadia McCaffrey, never saw the venomous black asp curled at her feet, until an enormous pain in her ankle drew her eyes downward.

"It stared through me like it was looking through my soul. I knew what had happened and I knew I was going to die," says Nadia. Screaming, she ran toward her grandmother, and as she reached her, passed out.

When she briefly came to, she could hear the doctors saying it was too late. "I understood, and I felt fine about it," says Nadia. Then she went into a coma for ten days, during which time she left her body, and looked down 'into it and at it.'

"It was horrible," says Nadia. "I didn't recognize myself because my left leg was the size of a tree, and the color of the snake.

It was brown, yellow and green because gangrene had started to set in at the sight of the bite."

Nadia could hear the doctor say that she'd have to have her leg amputated if she even survived. She found herself floating away from her body and being drawn to "a magnificent, beautiful Being of Light" who floated in the air by her side.

"She put her hands down and opened them and welcomed me," says Nadia. "This light was powerful and full of love. I felt like I wanted to curl up in her arms and stay there forever."

The being introduced herself to Nadia without speaking, but by conveying words to her with her mind. "I am your little mother in the sky," she told her. "You are not going to die. Don't be afraid. You'll be fine. You have a lot of things to do later on." The being assured Nadia that she would always be with her. Twice, she came to Nadia during her coma. The second time, she said, "It is time for us to separate, to depart. Never forget that love is all that counts. Always."

When Nadia came back to her body, at first she couldn't move her legs, although slowly over time, she managed to walk with a cane. Says Nadia, "It took me two months to reverse the damage, but no amputation was necessary. In six months, with no help from the medical world at all, I was back to normal, which was not possible according to the doctors."

By the time Nadia turned seventeen, the only thing she wanted to do was be with that loving Being of Light again that she had met in her coma, so she tried to commit suicide – twice. The first time, her stomach was pumped. The second time, she went unconscious.

"I left my body. It didn't interest me as the doctors pounded my chest, so I left that scene and was attracted by something else," says Nadia. "I knew that the light was on the other side. I was sucked – practically absorbed by it – to the other side. I was in the light. That's all I wanted."

However, this time, there was no loving presence to greet her. Suddenly, Nadia heard an enormous voice. "It sounded like thunder that came from everywhere and nowhere at the same time," says Nadia. The male voice declared, "You can't stay here. You haven't even begun your work yet." She was sent back.

As an adult, Nadia created two organizations called, "Changing the Face of Life," which helps people alleviate their fears around death, and "Angelstaff," where she teaches volunteers how to provide comfort and emotional support to those who are nearing their final hours.

One day, while sitting by the bedside of a woman in a coma, she, herself, began to feel ill. Within seconds, she had a fever of 105, and once again left her body.

"The chair was green and I was golden," says Nadia. "I knew I was going to the light again and I was happy about it. I left for another place, and in this place I was shown the past, the present and the future. It's another dimension. I knew where I was. There were different things from the earlier experience, but the light wasn't light though; it was golden and so was I. Very quickly, in front of my eyes flashed pictures of the past, and what was going on around the world – everything – the good, the bad, and two different possible futures for the world.

"One future is what we probably would call the Golden Age," says Nadia. "The other one looks like total destruction." Nadia saw herself in both futures. "In one, it's peaceful and I'm talking to people. The other is a huge dome and the sky and earth are red. The trees are dying or dead. People look gray and are suffering. I can see it and I can feel it. I live it. I am assisting people with food."

Nadia was led to understand that, as a society, we have a choice to go to one of these futures. "We have the power to raise our consciousness to a very high degree, and as we do so, we will influence others to do that as well, so that we will choose the right future," says Nadia.

She was also given a personal choice to consider: "I heard the same man's thunderous voice asking very loudly, 'Do you want to come Home?' I didn't answer because the future was flashing in front of my eyes. The voice repeated, 'Do you want to come Home now?' I said, 'No I can't leave now. I have so much work to do.'" Forty-eight hours later, she felt perfectly fine.

Miracle Thinking Tips

- Says Nadia, "When we do something not aligned with our Highest Good, we are stopped in our tracks by Divine Source." Being stopped in your tracks can look like an illness, an accident, or any disaster that turns your world upside down. When you are stopped in your tracks, open to the idea that, in time, a new and better way of being is going to be revealed to you.

- As a Miracle Thinker, "understand that you are here for a reason," says Nadia. "I know that I have chosen to come back here to do something specific, which is to help people through the process of life through death. I'm here to walk part of the path with other souls to bring them hope." Just as Nadia understands that she has a purpose, you have one, too.

* "If you want to be a Miracle Thinker, build your ability to love by living in it at all times. Just share this love. Love is the root of everything," says Nadia, who recently snuck into Iraq to sit with an Iraqi woman who had lost a son in the war just as her own son had been killed in Iraq. "Fill yourself with love and give it to the people around you. Also, be selfless. Service work is the answer for us to survive. Serve each other, love each other. That's what it's about."

"Imagine an Infinite Laser shaped like a pencil eraser, going back and forth, and erasing anything that shouldn't be around a particular organ."

– Norm Mosher

For Recovery from an Injury . . .

Zip It Up!

Blizzards in Connecticut are not the best time to be driving around a lake, however, Norm Mosher had important business to attend to. So, while most drivers were at home waiting for the violent snowstorm to subside, Norm had packed up his old Volvo and headed out. The visibility was so low, though, that there were hardly any vehicles on the road.

While rounding a corner, a patch of ice sent the Volvo barreling into the oncoming lane. At that exact moment, a truck came along and slammed head-on into Norm's vehicle. The truck then pushed the Volvo back about thirty feet before the trucker could bring his bulky machine to a stop. Horrified, the driver jumped out of the truck and raced over to the smashed up Volvo, the front of which was now about the size of a 12" Subway sandwich.

Much to his surprise, Norm was alive, although he was badly wounded and in shock. Still, Norm somehow had the sense to reach into the back seat of his car and gather the various items he might need to have with him while in the hospital. Then, while waiting for the ambulance to arrive, he applied the emergency training procedures he'd learned as a whitewater river guide in Maine, and scanned his body from head to toe to take count of his situation.

On the way to the hospital, one of the ambulance crew asked if he "wanted a blankie." and he responded in a child's voice, "Uh huh, and a teddy bear, too." The whole ambulance laughed, including Norm.

"You're not taking this very seriously," they reprimanded.

"If I take it seriously, it's gonna start hurting," came Norm's response.

As it turned out, a seatbelt, turtleneck, cable-knit sweater, and a thick leather jacket had not been enough to prevent the cracking of numerous ribs. His nose and one of his knees were broken, and his face had swollen to the size of a balloon. Meanwhile, numerous bleeding gashes outlined the top of his right eye and forehead.

Norm informed the Emergency Room doctor and nurses that he intended to go home after they finished taking x-rays and bandaging him up. Although the doctor strongly disapproved due to the state of his condition, he replied, "That's nice. I'm leaving anyway. I'll heal faster."

When his father came to pick him up, Norm hobbled out on his crutches to his father's car. His father then drove him back to his house where he remained positioned in a lounge chair for three days. He even had to sleep in the recliner because of his cracked knee. Since he couldn't get around, he decided to spend his time doing everything he could within his own power to heal himself. Of special concern were the three massive slices above his eyes, and the scarring that could result. So, he spent one to two hours at a time imagining that his cuts were healing.

"I remember visualizing that I was closing the gashes, just knowing that I would be able to heal them as quickly as I could focus on them," says Norm. "I started seeing them like a zipper closing right up. Then I'd look in the mirror at the side of my face that had no slices in it. I wanted to have a clear picture of what it would look like completely healed. I also declared, "I want no scarring."

Four days later, his friends were amazed. The gashes were gone. No scarring had occurred. They asked him "Did you WILL yourself to heal?" And he responded, "Yup!"

Miracle Thinking Tips

- As a Miracle Thinker, Norm declares: "The body is an amazing thing. It heals really quickly. If you want to heal yourself or others, don't see them as sick. See them as healthy. When you get a clear vision of what it is you want, that gives the universe something to aim for. The universe likes a good target."

- "Imagine an Infinite Laser shaped like a pencil eraser, going back and forth, and erasing anything that shouldn't be in, on, or around a particular organ. Then feel another healthy part of your body and say to the part you're healing, 'I want you to feel like this.' Or imagine a Giant Hand filled with light. As this Hand passes through your body, it has a net that grabs the things that are vibrationally wrong for you. See this Giant Hand taking these things away, moving them out of your body, and leaving only the pure "YOU" in its place." (Once any negative aspects are removed, fill the newly-healed parts with gold or white light).

* Miracle Thinkers also understand the value of humor to get through difficult moments. "It didn't really hit me until the next day. That's when I felt like I had been hit by a truck," says Norm who acknowledges that when the going gets rough, he gets humorous. "Laughter can take your mind off of pain or fear."

"The best way to manifest anything is to "place your order with the Cosmic Waitress," that Universal force which works to fulfill our dreams."

– Lila Harding

For Magical Manifesting...

The Cosmic Waitress

Moving away from the buzz of activity that surrounded her career as a marketing professional was the last thing on Lila Harding's mind. However, when she and her husband, Chris, fell in love with an area that was home to a holistic community of artists in Southern Utah, the two began to entertain thoughts of recreating their life in this remote region, which was situated a few hours away from their current residence.

Understanding the principles of manifestation, as Lila states, the best way to manifest anything is to "place your order with the Cosmic Waitress," that Universal force which works to fulfill our dreams. To "place their order" for their new living situation, first the couple decided to visualize what they wanted, then write out their list of goals, including as much detail as possible.

Shortly after completing their list, the Cosmic Waitress delivered a wonderful home. Situated to view the mammoth red rock cliffs that made the area famous, the home sat on over 2 acres of stunning, high-desert land, and featured hiking trails just outside the door.

Although the site clearly felt magical, the couple had a moment of hesitation, wondering if it might make more sense to rent for a year to see if the area was really right for them. However, after tossing the idea back and forth for a few days, they decided to make an offer on the property. Unfortunately, by the time they called the agent, they discovered that the house had just been sold.

Trusting that they would find the place that was right for them, they went ahead and gave notice to their landlord and continued to look. Soon afterwards, another house became available. The house would be suitable, but it lacked the magical feeling of that first home. Although they weren't in love with it, they decided to rent it anyway. However, just before signing their new lease, they learned that the house they'd originally wanted had just now come available for rent.

Rather than feeling ecstatic, however, doubt now crept in. Although the land surrounding the first house had that special magical feeling that they loved, there were still some issues of concern with the home itself. It was designed like a SoHo loft with a Santa Fe exterior. Strangely, not one of the three bathrooms contained a bathtub, and many of the rooms were round or configured awkwardly, which would make it impossible for their furniture to fit.

Lila made a detailed list of all of the pieces they would need to buy, and as she calculated the price, realized it would be very expensive to truly create the ambience they wanted. Lila felt torn. On one hand, they could rent this very nice home that, while lacking the magic, was a perfect place for their existing furniture. On the other hand, the original home with the magical feel to it would be expensive to transform into the kind of place they really wanted. Frustrated with her dilemma, Lila said to the Cosmic Waitress, "I just need some kind of sign. What should we do?"

Several days later, the Realtor greeted them with a smile. "I think we should go over to your favorite house again," he said. "You're going to be surprised." As he escorted Lila and Chris into the home, Lila gasped. The new owners had just furnished the home with custom-made furniture – from a gorgeous, round table in the kitchen, to special sofas, chairs, beds and carpets throughout the remaining areas. All of the furniture would come with the rental. Of course, the owners had never seen Lila's list or known of her dilemma; they'd furnished it with the idea of moving back some years later. However, the new furniture met all of Lila's exact specifications.

"I think you've got your sign," Lila's husband exclaimed. Lila and Chris moved into their magical desert home where they offer workshops on how to clarify intentions, manifest dreams, and place your order with the Cosmic Waitress!

Miracle Thinking Tips

* Says Lila, "The Cosmic Waitress will deliver whatever you want if you are clear about what you want and keep picturing it, focusing on it, and affirming it. When you make a list of what you want, include those intangible things, like the feelings you want to feel when you have those things. For example,

we had a brand new house with all the amenities, but I hadn't written down that we wanted it to feel magical. I just assumed that it would feel that way. It is necessary to state it."

* "We are manifesting all the time, but we often don't register that we're doing it, and when it appears we seldom recognize it. Notice what comes to you, and ask yourself, 'Did I put in a request for that?' Then recognize that you did. If something you've wanted, like a relationship or accomplishment, comes to you and you do not recognize it or it's not quite right, your picture probably wasn't clear to begin with. Don't be one of those tables who says, 'No, wait a minute. Can you change that again? The Cosmic Waitress will say, 'Chick, when you figure out what you want, put your order in and I'll bring you your food.'"

* "People talk about wanting to create abundance. The truth is that we already have an abundance of many things surrounding us in our lives. For example, we have an abundance of clothes in our closets, including outfits that we don't even wear. Instead of calling the process, 'creating abundance,' I call it, 'managing abundance.' Acknowledge what you already have, and include the people, relationships or communities in your life, which are also forms of abundance. Realize that you are totally rich."

"What labels do you wear as you recite your story to the world? Tell stories about yourself that uplift others."

– Susan Gilbert

The Phoenix

When David, a 19 year-old Marine from Pennsylvania, met 17 year-old Susan Gilbert at a dance, he knew in his heart that this was the girl he was going to marry. He asked Susan if he might call, and shortly thereafter the couple began to date.

Susan's parents approved of the young man. A perfect gentleman, he felt like the son they'd never had. Unfortunately, four months into their brief but serious courtship, he received orders to leave for Vietnam for thirteen months. Before he left, the young couple celebrated Christmas together and talked about getting engaged.

While in Vietnam, David wrote faithfully every day. He even had his picture taken by an Associated Press photographer, and had written Susan's name on his helmet. Susan lived in constant anxiety. If a day went by without a letter arriving, she would wonder whether or not he was still alive. Then the next day, when three letters would arrive, she would breathe a huge sigh of relief.

As his tour of duty in Viet Nam was coming to an end, David learned that he would be stationed in California for one more year. Upon his return, the couple married and moved across country. By the end of the year, however, David couldn't wait to move back to Pennsylvania. Meanwhile, Susan had fallen in love with their new locale. Since the military had offered to move the couple back to Pennsylvania for up to a year after his discharge, they decided to wait eleven more months. If David could find good work, they would stay, if not, they would go back.

Eleven months later, they moved back East, where he attended college and became a Penn State Police Officer. Then, during a routine checkup for what he thought was a cold, the doctors delivered some shocking news. David had a rare and acute form of leukemia; he was given just two weeks to live. (Years later, it became obvious that as a machine gunner on a helicopter, he had been exposed to Agent Orange numerous times. He had even written about it. However, in 1975, the effects of the chemical rainfall were not known.)

Susan and her family were totally distraught. Meanwhile, Susan's mother was also admitted to the same hospital where David now resided. Surgery revealed an aggressive form of cancer, which had spread to her liver.

Both her mother and husband were being cared for by the same doctors. Susan spent her days shuffling back and forth between the two floors where the two people she loved the most in the world lay dying.

Her twenty-eight year old husband passed away first. When Susan asked the doctors if she could bring her mother home for the funeral, she was told that since the chemotherapy and radiation weren't working, her mother might as well be kept at home since there was nothing more they could do. She died four months later.

"I lost the two people that I was the closest to in the world," says Susan. "My mother was only 51. You don't expect to lose both a spouse and a parent when you are twenty-five. I wasn't prepared financially. We didn't have life insurance or hospitalization. My husband was three credits away from graduating. The plan was that he'd get his college education first, then I would get mine. I had no income. I had no education. There was no money to pay the bills."

In her small hometown, everyone sadly called her, "the young widow." Susan realized that she would either have to resign herself to accepting that label, or take one step to move forward in her life.

Susan chose to take that one step, which was to head back to California. "I believed that I had a responsibility to really live, because after seeing the two people that I loved die painful deaths, I felt like I had a responsibility to make the most out of my life."

Since she wasn't quite sure what she wanted to do, she decided to take a general aptitude test at a California university. She learned that she had good communication skills and 3-D spatial skills, indicating she would make either a good attorney or architect. All she felt, though, was disappointment since she had no interest in either of those occupations.

As she walked out to her car, a woman abruptly stopped her in the parking lot and blurted out, "Have you ever thought of sales?" Susan eyed the woman suspiciously. Although they had been in the same class, the two had not exchanged one word during the entire weekend course. Was she a crazy person?

The woman proceeded to tell Susan that her husband had opened up a computer store and that his staff consisted entirely of men. Her husband wanted to hire a woman, and she believed that Susan would be great for the job.

"This was the '70's," says Susan. "In my mind, computers were monstrous machines kept in great big rooms. I thought she was nuts. Besides, didn't all salesmen wear polyester suits and work in used car lots?"

Two weeks later, Susan decided to call the woman's husband, and was pleasantly surprised by his natural warmth. "He showed me what a computer looked like. It was the predecessor to the IBM PC and it took up the whole desk."

Susan accepted his offer, and rather than explaining the inner workings of a hard drive, as her male cohorts were doing, she began to show people how to use them. Her new boss was thrilled, proclaiming, "Susie, you're a natural."

Thus began Susan's new career and direction. Her success kept multiplying upon itself. "When the IBM PC came out, I did very well," says Susan. "Then when I divested, I was hired by AT&T to head up their national data sales organization for selling PCs."

With the earnings from her career, Susan eventually started her own business, opening a café in the heart of San Diego. She also wrote a book to help others move beyond those places in their lives where they felt stuck.

"I live my life as an adventure," says the woman who believes that "to be fearless is to fear less and to move. I was catapulted into a situation where there was no place to go but up. I had lost everything. When you have lost everything and you build and begin anew, you know that even if you lose everything again, you can do it all over again."

Miracle Thinking Tips

* Tell stories about yourself that uplift others. When you talk about yourself, do you focus on your losses or personal drama? Says Susan, "Like the phoenix, I'd been disassembled and I had to reassemble myself. I moved across country and gained a new identity where no one would think of me as 'the young widow. Don't wear your losses like your own personal label."

* Susan identifies stuck places as: "the Land of Apathy, where life feels dull and habitual; the Land of Fear, where one feels afraid to face an unknown future; the Land of Sorrow, where we experience loss, and the Land of Ashes, where everything dissolves before we begin anew." She also speaks of the Land of I Can, where the "I" stands for your imagination, intention, and intuition, and the "CAN" stands for Commitment, Action, and do it Now. "Focus on your end result. See your success and put your emotions into it," she says. "I imagined a better life. I saw myself successful and upbeat. If I want to make a change now, like losing ten pounds, I don't think about losing the weight. I focus on how fun it will be to get into my new outfit and how sexy I'll feel when I do it."

➤ "Just take one step and don't worry about creating the end result. I didn't know how to build another life, but I had a vision that there was a better life in store for me, and the only way for me to create that life would be to move away from the old one. Use your power of visualization, take action, and create movement. That's where the magic is."

"When crisis calls, state with as much power as you possibly can that 'this is temporary'."

– Linda Peterson

For Reinventing Yourself . . .

Becoming the Diamond

Linda Peterson was in her early 20's when she was recruited by the president of a Baptist seminary to become a minister. This was a radical step for the entirely conservative seminary, but it was the '80's and the church was making strides to be more inclusive. Besides, Linda's husband was also studying to be a minister, so she seemed like a good candidate.

Although Linda enjoyed her academic classes, she found herself challenging every theological fundamental presented. Still, her personal faith had always been strong, and she pursued the ordination, regardless of the fact that the administration was becoming more and more intimidated by the young woman who had her own beliefs about things.

When her marriage eventually soured and divorce was eminent, Linda, who by this time had been ordained, applied for clergy positions within the Denver area where she lived. However, as a divorced clergy person, who also happened to be a woman, she was not welcomed anywhere. Her husband, on the other hand, had been offered a position even though he was not yet ordained.

After a few months of problems with her ex-spouse concerning the financial support of her children, Linda decided there was no good reason to remain in the area. But where would she go with two children under age three and barely any money? She called her parents, who abruptly said, "You got yourself into this. You get yourself out of it." With no plan in mind or prearranged destination, she packed up the car, loaded her two boys into their car seats, and headed east.

Days later, her car died right outside a military base in Devon, Massachusetts. Coincidentally, Linda had completed her seminary internship on a military base as a hospital chaplain. So, she walked onto the army installation and immediately talked herself into a job as a social worker with a Special Forces division. Wandering around the perimeter of the base, she then found an abandoned building and secretly moved her little family into it.

"We were basically homeless. It was February. The building had no heat or electricity. I had my kids in full time child care through a program for single mothers, which was subsidized by the State. This program ensured that my children had two hot meals a day. Three nights a week we ate at a soup kitchen," says Linda.

Simultaneously, Linda experienced a temporary crisis in her faith, feeling like she was being "tested to the max. My parents had always been uninvolved in my life. I used to tell people 'I was raised by wolves.' I felt abandoned by my alcoholic mother as a child, and now I felt like God had abandoned me as an adult. I wrote and poured my heart out to God in my journal, and I wondered why I was so unlovable. Ultimately, though, I knew that God would sustain us."

In time, the military police figured out that Linda and her boys were taking refuge in the abandoned building. Initially, they sympathetically dropped off blankets and food, but as the weather worsened, one of the MPs went to the Colonel Supervisor out of concern and reported the situation. The Colonel Supervisor immediately contacted the director of the church Linda had begun attending. What were the odds that a member of the church had just purchased a Victorian house and happened to be looking for a tenant? Linda and her children were able to move in without having to provide a security deposit.

Two years later, when her contract on base was coming to an end, she was invited to continue her practice on a military base in Berlin. Her children, however, would not be allowed to go. Obviously, this was not going to be an option. What next?

A ruptured ovary was certainly not among Linda's plans. However, the unexpected health crisis sent her kids to live with their dad for a summer. Although Linda's parents never called, her grandmother stepped in and encouraged her to move to California where she lived. Linda didn't have the money or desire to make such a move, but when her grandmother offered to pay for their relocation, Linda heard something in her grandmother's voice that sounded like she needed her.

Selling everything she had accumulated in Massachusetts, she arrived in California with her two little boys and four suitcases. At first sight, the remote town in which her grandmother lived appeared to be "God forsaken." She was sure that she'd just blundered into making "another poor life decision." However, with money lent to her by her grandmother, she began to sell Mary Kay cosmetics, and within a short period of time, created a thriving business.

She also managed to locate a job as a Hospice social worker. One day, a man who was visiting her small town was admitted to the local hospital. This was 1985, and he was the hospital's first AIDS patient. Fear ran rampant throughout the facility. A public health doctor called Linda and said, "I've heard your name come up in the medical community and I'm wondering if you'd work with this guy?" Immediately, Linda jumped into her car and sped off to the hospital.

When she arrived, the first thing she saw was a tray of food sitting on a paper placemat on the floor. Linda wanted to go into the man's room, but was told she couldn't without a gown to protect herself. She went in anyway, and proceeded to work with him.

"My kids weren't allowed to go to school because their mother worked with an AIDS patient," says Linda, "and the Board of Hospice asked for my resignation. They were concerned about their funding and working with 'those kinds of people.'"

Eventually, the man was well enough to leave the hospital, and Linda invited him to stay with her family for a time. She never experienced the kind of terror that many people felt about AIDS back in the '80's. "I was never terrified because I'd think that these were the same people who Jesus ministered to," she says. "I once worked a summer job as a Nurse's Aid in a nursing home. I was grossed out by the smells. But I learned to look at each one of the residents as someone who had a story and who was loved by God. That helped me to deliver a high quality of care. I set aside all of my fears for humanity. I believe we're called to be a light and a healing presence in these kinds of environments, and we have to show up in that kind of powerful way. That's just the way it is."

After Linda resigned from Hospice, she created an AIDS support network, and developed a comprehensive AIDS program for her county. Eventually, she remarried, moved to Northern California, worked in a church, then re-divorced. All along, she continued to sell Mary Kay products, which enabled her to put both of her sons through college. Wanting to connect with other business people, she eventually joined a local chapter of a national business networking organization, and in time was offered a position as its Regional Executive Director.

From mom, to pioneer for women in the seminary, to hospital chaplain, to minister, to homeless person, to social worker, to Mary Kay distributor, to AIDS activist, to minister again, to director of a networking organization, Linda has had to reinvent herself many times.

Laughing, she says, "I have had so many different public personas. I feel like a piece of coal that, through the force of the earth, has become the diamond." She believes that we are all 'diamonds in the rough.' "It's not just the diamond," she says, "but it's the jeweler who knows how to take that rough diamond and find all of its beautiful facets. I believe that God is the Master Jeweler. All of the circumstances of our lives can be chiseled if we are open."

Miracle Thinking Tips

- When life presents overwhelming odds, you might feel like your situation is going to last forever. In reality, your difficulty is only happening in this moment for as long as this moment lasts. "What has always sustained me is feeling some sense of hope," says Linda. "Even in my deepest, darkest times, I had hope that God was walking with me through this valley, that I was not alone, and that somehow this was going to be temporary. It's not forever. That takes away the fear." All moments are subject to change. When crisis calls, state with as much power as you can that "this is temporary."

- How do we change our moments? "Through the power of our thoughts, and through prayer, action, surrender and gratitude. If we hold the belief that we can change our reality, we have the power to create a new reality," says Linda. "It's all about choice. Some people become embittered by life's experiences or feel like victims. I have never been a victim. I realize that I have personal choices. I made a choice when I married my first husband, when I drove east, and when I worked with AIDS patients. I take responsibility for my choices."

- "There's the saying, 'When God closes a door he always opens a window.' I truly believe that. Every time I've had to reinvent myself and a door has closed, a window has been opened. I'm an optimistic person. I see things as lessons we can learn from. The main lesson I've learned is that I have intrinsic value and worth. God created me, just like God creates all of us, with incredible value and worth." Do you recognize your value and worth?

"Tell your home you love living in it; your car how much you appreciate its good running order; and your clothes how beautiful they make you feel."

– Suzka

A Garden Full of Miracles

Growing up in the Mid-West, Suzka could not recall a time when her family didn't have a hearty vegetable garden growing during the summer months. As a young girl, every evening before dinner she would run outside to pick the bounty of the day, which might include anything from a giant head of fresh leaf lettuce, to a bunch of tomatoes and carrots, or a bag full of green beans.

Suzka's father was an excellent gardener and his love of gardening was evident. In fact, every seed he planted grew into an enormous, lush plant.

One day, Suzka overheard her father talking out loud in his little green house in the backyard. Knowing he was by himself, she was puzzled.

"Dad, who are you talking to?" she asked quizzically.

"My babies," he replied.

"Your babies? I don't see any babies."

"The baby plants," he responded. "I talked to their parents, and see how big they have gotten? If I talk to the babies, they too, will grow as big and as beautiful."

Suzka never forgot her father's response. Years later, she moved to Oregon, where she purchased a wonderful house with a big yard. Unfortunately, her yard was filled with muddy clay, which would make it almost impossible for vegetables to grow.

As spring approached, she began to level the land, and slowly, a yard filled with shrubs, plants and grass took shape. However, a clay-filled patch of the yard near her house remained untouched, and Suzka watched as the weeds rallied together and took over that spot.

One day, she started to talk to them. "How can you grow in this clay? Look at how big you are." As she proceeded to talk to the weeds, they grew incredibly tall. She admired their beauty. "I would pick the Queen's Anne Lace to decorate my table," says the nature lover who couldn't understand why weeds had such a negative connotation. "So many of them are quite lovely," she says. "They don't require much care and they just grow and grow."

As the years passed, Suzka continued to visit the little patch and talk lovingly to her weeds. One day, she decided it was time to make her dream of having a vegetable garden come true. As she began to pull up the weeds, at first she was saddened to think that she was destroying their home. Then she realized that perhaps they had grown as large as they had in order to show her that this would be a great place for her garden. After all, if the weeds could grow under such adverse conditions when she talked to them, couldn't a garden do the same?

Meanwhile, Suzka's neighbor labored over his own vegetable garden. After roto-tilling the earth, he fertilized the land, applied insecticides, and watered his fledgling plants. Woefully, he looked at Suzka's garden patch and said, "Nothing is going to grow there. You don't get but an hours' worth of sun a day."

Suzka replied, "Well, we'll see. I have a plan."

As the months passed, Suzka's garden flourished. Actually, to say that her garden flourished might be an understatement, as the tomato plants were at least 12 feet high and were loaded with fruit.

The neighbor gawked in awe. One day, while she was out picking the fruit, he commented over the fence, "Wow! You must be using a great fertilizer. My tomatoes don't look nearly as good as yours even though they're getting sun all day. You're only getting an hour of sun. What's your secret?"

"Well, I talk to them. I call it 'plant chats.' I give them words of encouragement to grow big and strong. And then, I hug them."

Laughingly, he replied, "You won't see me doing that!"

Suzka remembered her conversation with her father in his greenhouse. "If you love your plants, and talk to them and hug them, they will love you back by growing big and beautiful." Every year now, Suzka has hundreds of tomatoes showing her their love in the clay-filled patch where nothing should ever have grown.

Miracle Thinking Tips

- ❀ We cannot underestimate the power of love in having an effect upon all things. If you want to grow plants that bare lush vegetables, fruits or flowers, love them. If you want your pets and animals to thrive, love them. If you want your spouse, partner or children to blossom, love them.

- The power of love runs deeper than we realize. If you want your home to be a place where you feel nurtured, tell your home how much you love living in it, and how you feel so nurtured when you are there. If you want your car to run, love it. Tell your car how much you appreciate it for staying in such good running order and keeping you safe. If you want to look beautiful, tell your clothes how beautiful they make you feel when you wear them.

- Bestow your love upon all things, both animate and inanimate. The more you love, the more the universe bestows love upon you in all its many forms. Remember to love yourself as well. There is no end to this love, and it is only love that will sustain us in the end.

"Designate a space where you can meditate. As you get quiet, your deepest desires will surface. From this place, ask the Universe for what you want."

– Una Versailles

For Asking for a Sign . . .

The Pencil

Una Versailles was at a crossroads in her career. Although she'd dreamt about writing a book for years, she was a practical person who knew that once she left her work as a technical writer, she would be hard-pressed to recreate the kind of financial security that her steady paycheck had provided for 22 years. Still, she knew that something had to change because she was so burnt out that the idea of continuing to work in the technical writing field made her physically ill.

One day, she sat quietly in meditation and declared to the Universe, "I need to know exactly what it is I am supposed to be doing next. Can I really just write a book, and give up technical writing and the income that goes with it? I need a sign. I've gotten some wonderful signs in the past, but this time I want it to be really clear and unambiguous." Not having any expectations about what might result, she moved on with her day and forgot about her request.

Early the next morning, she left her house to walk to a 12-Step meeting that she had attended for several years. En route, she spotted a big, brightly colored object lying on the ground. From a distance, she couldn't quite tell what the strange-looking object was. As she approached it, she discovered that she was staring down at a giant orange pencil. It was sixteen inches long and more than an inch in diameter; it even had a sharpened tip.

Not recognizing that the Universe had just provided her with a rather large sign, Una left the pencil lying where it was. Perhaps someone had just dropped it and would come back for it. On her return trip, however, she realized that the pencil was the sign she'd been looking for. Obviously, it meant that she should start writing her book. She brought the pencil home, let go of her career as a technical writer, and joyfully dove into her new project. Simultaneously, she discovered that her home had appreciated so much that she was able to receive an equity line of credit that would help meet all of her financial needs for the time being.

Whenever she dips into a moment of fear about her financial future, she looks at the giant pencil and remembers how it came to her. "Whether it's divine coincidence or a direct answer to a miracle, I don't care," she says. "It's okay for me not to know how the world works. I just know there is something going on that I don't understand, and I'm going to rely on that 'something' to take care of me while I'm in this transition."

Trust is the most important factor for Una. "I trust myself more. I no longer think that I'm doing something wrong if I don't feel wonderful, perfect, happy or ecstatic every minute. That's not realistic. But I do have a sense of peace that is strong enough so that when I feel fearful, it doesn't last very long. This may turn out to be a big, silly experiment, but I know I'll learn something," she says. "I can't tell what the future is going to bring, but I never missed a meal . . . even when I tried hard. I'm very resourceful and I do trust that my faith will carry me through."

Miracle Thinking Tips

- "Create a practice for yourself that feeds your spiritual hunger," says Una. "Whether you choose a spiritual study group, 12-Step meetings, daily readings, service to others, Yoga, or anything else that feeds your soul, develop the habit of nurturing that part of your life. You'll develop the kind of self-discipline that can only make your life better. When your spiritual life is in good shape, everything else is easier; when it is not in good shape, nothing else will fill your longing for that sacred connection."

- Una also advises to designate a special space in your home or in nature where you can meditate. "Get quiet and give yourself complete permission not to think about anything," she says. "You don't have to worry when you're sitting there. You don't need to keep a list of what you're supposed to be doing that day. You don't have to solve any problems. Just sit there and be completely quiet." As you get quiet, your deepest desires will surface. From this place, ask the Universe for what you want, then let it go, and be open to see how your request is answered.

✦ Also notice where you focus your attention. Says Una, "Feelings are not facts. Painful or fearful emotions go through you; they're temporary. You get to decide whether you want to take your feelings and fan the flames, or whether you want to just notice them and say, 'I'm just feeling this way right now.'"

"If you can listen to your TV for hours on end, can you now apply those same listening skills to listen to your Spirit within?"

– Randy Peyser

A Miracle from Above

Anyone who is familiar with New Orleans knows that come September, the temperature often hits 97 and the humidity factor races to 100 per cent. With no air-conditioning, Adano Henderson's kindergarten classroom felt like a sauna. The only source of relief came from two giant, 150-pound, commercial fans which swung high overhead in the middle of the classroom.

Usually, four 'lucky' children got to sit right underneath the fans, and thereby, receive the benefit of the coolest possible air stream. However, on this day, Adano was so hot, she felt like she was burning up. First, she went to the Women's Room to remove her stockings, but the sweat continued to pour off of her so badly, that finally, she moved the four kids who sat under the fans, and put her chair in their place.

Even after situating herself under the giant fans, Adano continued to feel the blazing heat, which just seemed to be getting worse and worse. At one point, she got up from her chair and walked to one side of the room. All of a sudden, one of the big 150 lb. fans came crashing to the ground. Her chair splintered into a thousand pieces. Not only were Adano and the children safe, but the unbearable heat immediately lifted.

Miracle Thinking Tips

* Guidance can come in forms that we fail to recognize, yet we are always being led. Says Adano, "No one can tell me to this day that that wasn't the Holy Spirit on me. I had moved my children. If they had stayed under the fan they would have been killed. I could have been underneath it also, but I wasn't. After it fell, I was shaking, but I no longer felt hot. I realized that nothing but the Holy Spirit led me to remove those children."

* To more consciously tune into your guidance, simply ask that it be so, then learn how to listen so that you can receive the guidance that is being given to you. Most of us have mastered our ability to listen from years of watching television. Now that the TV has helped us to develop our capacity to listen, we can apply our listening skills to tune in and begin to listen to the Spirit within. Can you imagine what your life might be like if you focused in on Spirit in the same way that you've allowed yourself to focus in on television programs for all of these years?

➴ You can never underestimate the power of living in one's truth. Adano demonstrated this universal principle when it was her truth that she was so hot that she simply *had* to remove the four children's desks in the middle of the room and put her chair in their place to cool herself down. By taking care of herself in that manner, Adano was living in her truth in that moment. As a result, her life, and the lives of the four children who sat under the fan, were saved.

"When you feel challenged, ask yourself, 'what small piece of the larger picture can I accomplish today'?"

– Betty Anne Sayers

There's No Place Like Home

Since their mom was now in her eighties, Betty Anne Sayers and her sister, Nancy Herhahn, decided it made sense to move back home to their roots. But what would the dreary Midwest have to offer the writer who had a busy social life in Minnesota, or her go-get'em sister who had a fabulous job as a Vice President for a major corporation in San Diego? Wouldn't moving home to the barren plains of Nebraska be a giant step backward in both cases? Still, for the sake of their elderly mother, they decided to pack up their lives and return.

Within a short period of time, however, the two discovered that the area, which they thought might bore them to tears, was its own piece of heaven. "There's so much emptiness, you can see the curve of the earth and you can see the stars at night," says Betty. In addition to its physical charm, the two discovered that Nebraska also held an entirely different appeal. Says Betty, "One of Nebraska's mottos is 'endless possibilities.' When you come out here, there's no script. You can write your own script. We asked ourselves, 'What are we going to invent so that we can step out and be fully alive and be engaged in life?' "

As Betty and Nancy began to brainstorm their new script, they thought about the strengths each one possessed. For example, Betty liked to tell stories, while Nancy enjoyed working with data. Would there be some way their interests might intersect?

The two began to research their new locale, and with Nancy's penchant for data, they noted the high graduation rates, and the number of students who went on to further their education and graduated. The numbers were exceptionally high, in the 99 percentiles. However, in spite of those statistics, as much as 20% of the population was continually moving elsewhere.

Continuing their research, they repeatedly heard the dire reports about the drought and the terrible economy. On the other hand, life on the prairie was like something out of a Norman Rockwell painting; rows of kid's bikes were left at the swimming pool with no locks on them, and there was a sense of safety and security in the area that one would be hard-pressed to find elsewhere – never mind the cost of housing, where $36,000 would purchase the equivalent of a $350,000 home in Chicago.

"We asked ourselves, 'what can we do to give this area the attention it deserves, and maybe even bring people back'?" says Betty. The sisters decided to start a 'Bring Your Own Back Home' campaign. After receiving a grant from the USDA for $25,000 and some small funding from the little towns in the area, they found an office to rent for $50 a month, and started creating an online high school alumni association, which would cover 800 miles of Nebraska prairie.

Quickly, they discovered that everybody knew someone who was somewhere. In a short time, they had a database with the names of 7500 Nebraskans, all of whom now lived out of the region, and at least one of whom lived in every country around the world. The relatives of those who left the area couldn't be happier about the sisters' program with the prospect of possibly having their loved ones return.

Betty is intent upon preserving the culture of the area that has captured her heart. "It's all one of a kind," she says. "While there are chain stores in the bigger towns, the little towns still have home cooking and oatmeal pie. Did you ever hear of such a thing? It's like pecan pie and it's really good."

On a daily basis, Betty witnesses little miracles as she interviews the locals in all the tiny towns. "Globalization hasn't totally destroyed the character of the immigrants here," she says. "For example, there is a woman who became the village pie maker. She used a pie crust recipe that was her great grandmother's. She began making these frozen fruit pies and people liked them. So she decided to sell them at the truck stops along the I-80 corridor. Then she opened up a darling little store. Just last week, she received an order from a company in Chicago for 2000 pies a month. She's going to have to add more room and hire help. It was just her and the guy who drove the pies around."

In addition to helping to revitalize their region, the two are reaping many personal benefits they never could have foreseen. Says Betty, "I left Minnesota, where I saw eagles, deer and fox every day. Yet, every bit of stuff I bought was through a catalog or over the Internet. Today, if I buy anything, I want somebody to know who I am and why I bought it from them. I want them to talk to me about it. I don't want to give my money to somebody I don't know or don't care about. I want connection."

The sisters now buy everything for their business locally from their region. "If we can't buy it in this region, we don't get it. Our business is here and this is where our relationships are."

The sisters' project has drawn the attention of newspapers, from small town presses to USA Today. "We are now at the place where a marketing firm is developing photos to mail to all of our alumni with an invitation to look at our web site," says Betty. "It's amazing. It's coming together and it's really working."

Miracle Thinking Tips

* Create a foundation of hope by focusing on what is working, rather than by focusing on your problems. Betty Anne writes stories about the communities throughout her region, but she won't write about anything that's not positive. "I only want to hear about what is working, because focusing on what is working expands creativity, which then breeds hope." Children also enrich her feelings of hope, as do "wildflowers, birds, 13-striped gophers, and the 10,000 other beings that populate the wilderness," she says.

* "If you are pursuing your dream, hold the view that people are giving and that they genuinely want to help you. They say that the sixth person you tell your story to is the one who will say, 'I want to do that,' and then they'll just show up and do whatever it is you wanted. That's what we've been counting on

and it seems like it is working. We're constantly telling our story, and then all at once, we'll hear from someone who will say, 'here's some people who have alumni names,' or 'here's a check for fifty dollars.' "

* Work for a larger good. Betty and Nancy see their work as being of benefit to their entire region, however, they've discovered that each community views itself in competition with its neighbors; after all, their high school football teams have been rivals for decades. "We're trying to change that competitive view point by reminding everybody that we are one world; first, we are a region, and what helps one helps the next. What we give to one another benefits all. That's a different way of looking at things."

"Stay open to all possibilities. Otherwise you may be waiting impatiently at the airport when your ship comes in loaded with treasure."

– Karen Williams

For Finding Your Soul Mate . . .

The Match
Made in Heaven

By the time she had reached mid-life, Karen Williams had kissed several frogs, as well as a few toads. Although "Mr. Soul Mate" had not shown up at the single's group she had attended, nor via the Internet, she refused to give up hope that, one day, she would have a life partner.

At the same time, she had many interests that kept her happily fulfilled – from freelance writing, to the study of spirituality and hands-on healing, to the care and feeding of a teenage daughter. Although she acknowledged that "having a partner would be fabulous," her life was, at many levels, already deeply satisfying.

In time, through the sharing of metaphysical interests, Karen became friends with a woman named, Ellie, and her husband, Mark. Observing Ellie and Mark reminded Karen of just how meaningful a love relationship could be. The couple seemed to adore each other. Watching the lovebirds also helped Karen to define the qualities of loyalty, respect, and taking delight in another's presence, which were all qualities she would want to have in a partnership some day.

Shockingly, two years down the road, Ellie suddenly decided to leave Mark to return to her previous calling as an itinerant spiritual healer. Deeply saddened, Mark wondered where he'd gone wrong. He had always supported Ellie in her various efforts, including the creation of a shop where she'd sold metaphysical items and given readings.

Hoping to become a catalyst in reuniting her friends, Karen held various phone conversations with each. Ellie remained adamant, however, and filed for divorce. In the following weeks, Karen's and Mark's conversations about the mystery that was Ellie broadened to include other topics, especially their methods of staying mentally positive no matter what life dished out. Little by little, over time, Karen and Mark found themselves experiencing more than mere friendship.

When Ellie who was by now several hundred miles away, learned of their connection, she immediately decided to return to Mark. (Hello, human nature!) Months of turbulence followed, culminating in Mark and Ellie finally agreeing to go their separate ways.

Mark, who loves to encourage people's metaphysical meanderings, proceeded to build Karen a website as home base for her inspirational e-mails that she sends out worldwide. He also helped her publish her first book, which was the fulfillment of Karen's long-held desire to share her writings in book form.

Meanwhile, Karen, a compulsive organizer who would rather file papers than eat, found plenty of paperwork waiting for her at Mark's business. To Karen and Mark, their relationship seems to be the proverbial match made in heaven. Even Ellie, who is now busy with her new endeavors, grudgingly agrees.

Miracle Thinking Tips

- "If you want to manifest long-held desires, remain as relaxed and happy as possible where you are right now in your life. Holding desires while appreciating current circumstances opens the doors to the manifestation of your dreams," Karen asserts.

- "Stay as peaceful as possible when things appear to be falling apart," she continues. When Ellie re-entered Mark's life, determined to end his and Karen's connection, Karen dealt with uncertainty and anxiety by regularly clearing her mind through meditation and clinging to the belief that "well-being is the overall theme of the Universe."

- Karen also advocates staying mentally flexible. "The Universe has countless surprising tricks up its sleeve to help us manifest the life we really want," she says. "Stay open to all possibilities. Otherwise you may be waiting impatiently at the airport when your ship comes in loaded with treasure."

"I talk straight to God. I'll say, 'I am open to receiving perfect guidance about what I need to know now. What is my next step on my healing path?"

– Rayna Lumbard

Take Back Your Power

Although Rayna Lumbard was happily married with a darling son, for over 20 years she searched for the answer as to why she never felt quite right. Plagued with bouts of depression, exhaustion, and a general feeling of imbalance in her body, she constantly sought the expertise of medical doctors and holistic health providers. In spite of the many tests and numerous health regimens she tried over the years, no one was able to help her identify the source of her symptoms.

As a licensed Marriage and Family Therapist and psychospiritual healer, Rayna couldn't help but see the irony of her situation. Although she was able to empower others to heal themselves, she herself lived in what felt like constant struggle as she tried to maintain her own sense of well being and harmony.

One day during meditation, Rayna again turned to God for help with her health issues. She began to relax and open to what she calls 'God's infinite love and wisdom' when, all of a sudden, she heard a voice. Clear as a bell, this voice said, "Go have a Hepatitis C test." In all her years of searching for clues, not one medical or holistic practitioner had ever suggested this test. Sure enough, when Rayna went to her medical doctor and was tested, she discovered that she did, indeed, have Hepatitis C.

All of the symptoms she'd been experiencing for most of her adult life finally made sense. How had she contracted the disease? Probably from having been a dental hygienist from 1972 to 1984. She guessed that she must have come in contact with contaminated blood, since before the AIDS epidemic in the early '80's, very few in the dental profession protected themselves with latex, masks and glasses.

On one level, Rayna felt a sense of relief. She finally had a diagnosis that explained why she had felt poorly for so many years. But when she began reading about the recommended medical treatment and all of the scary things that could happen as a result of having Hep C, she quickly catapulted herself from relief into terror and anger. Why would God reveal this information to her now when the Hep C had been causing damage to her liver for over twenty years?

Although feeling highly charged, Rayna believed that if she allowed herself to stay in this intense state of fear and upset, she would never heal; if she wanted to heal, she would need answers, and to find them she knew she had to take back her power.

Again in meditation, she asked herself many questions: How can I take control of my health and life? What am I learning from this? How can I get my power back? Then she stayed open for the answers and insights to present themselves. One answer she heard was "make friends with your body. Listen to it." So she began to ask her body questions. "What do I need to eat to heal you (my body)? What do I need to drink? What else do you (body) truly need and want?"

Rayna learned how to discern what her body truly needed and wanted, from the desires of an insistent 'inner child' who craved sugary treats that wouldn't support her body's health. She figured out which foods would benefit her in her healing process and which foods were detrimental. She incorporated daily exercise and therapeutic baths along with her continual emotional release work and meditation. As a result, her health rebounded significantly.

Through this experience, she has learned to trust her own intuition, rather than rely on the advice of others – especially from those who call themselves experts. Today, whenever different therapies, whether traditional or complementary, are suggested, she asks herself, "Which path is going to lead me closer to my goal of perfect health now?" By asking such questions, then staying open to hear her answers, Rayna continues to discover the types of healing modalities and the timing for each that will best serve her.

Although Hep C is a chronic virus that remains dormant in the body for years before showing any outward symptoms, Rayna doesn't see herself as having a chronic problem. Instead, quite vibrantly, she exclaims, "I see myself reducing the viral count to zero and being totally victorious!"

"When one feels fear, one also feels powerless. I won't give my power up to any condition or anybody anymore," says Rayna. "I thought the doctors and holistic practitioners knew what they were doing, but no one really found the core of my imbalance for twenty years. Now I'm more in charge of my own healthcare than ever. I know I can heal this. I am going through an incredible metamorphosis, and I thank God everyday for this opportunity to truly heal myself and move on in my life."

Miracle Thinking Tips

* "When you face a health challenge or condition, make a conscious decision to be victorious, not a victim of your circumstances," says Rayna. "Know that you are a powerful healing force, and that you can access your confidence and inner strength to deal positively with any situation by remembering other challenges that you have overcome. Ask your family, friends, and health providers to be part of your support system and healing team. Trust that you are learning what you need to learn from this experience, and that good is coming out of it for yourself and others, even if you don't know exactly what that will look like."

* Take responsibility for healing yourself through meditation. Learn to relax your body, then breathe deeply as you calm your mind and feelings and go into meditation. Ask questions and be open to listen so that you are ready to intuitively receive any answers or insights coming from your higher self or spiritual guidance. Says Rayna, "I go into meditation and call in my highest spiritual healing guides, including the dolphins and angels, to rally around me. Then I talk straight to God. I'll say, 'I am open

to receiving perfect guidance about what I need to know now. What is my next step on my healing path? Which supplement will be best for me? Between these two practitioners, which one will be the most helpful in being my health partner?' Then I listen in between the questions to hear the answers and to feel that gut feeling that tells me, 'Yes I need to go with that.'"

"In order to be clear enough to hear your answers, first you've got to release your emotional pain – including any feelings of terror, frustration, anger, despair, fear, grief, sadness or anxiety you are carrying. Discover your core feelings by having a crying session, seeing a therapist, or doing whatever it takes to clear yourself. Then get into a calm and receptive space. Only when you are calm and clear will you be able to hear the input that you receive. Once you receive that input, ask inwardly if that input is right for you."

"When you face a scary unknown, set strong, clear boundaries as to what you are willing or not willing to accept as part of your experience."

– JJ Crow

For Dealing with a Life-Threatening Condition . . .

Dispensing Miracles

Life had always felt difficult for JJ Crow. On top of a history of disastrous relationships, financial upheaval, and other health challenges, she had just now discovered a suspicious lump in her breast. After making an appointment with her doctor, she soon found herself facing a lumpectomy. Unfortunately, when the procedure failed to remove all of the malignancy, radiation and chemotherapy were a necessity in her doctor's opinion.

Adamantly, however, JJ declared to the M.D., "No way. I'm not putting myself through radiation and chemo. I've already had enough pain in my life. This is not an option." Then she went home to think about how she might have attracted a breast lump into her life experience.

As she thought about it, she recognized that throughout her entire life, in the back of her mind, she always said to herself, 'Life's too hard. I don't want to be here.' She realized that if she continued to think this way, her negative belief might become a self-fulfilling prophecy. JJ decided to immediately do a 'course-correction' and "embrace life on life's terms. I made a conscious decision to choose life," she says.

A year later, she returned to her doctor. The mass had grown much larger. This time, more than a lumpectomy would be necessary. After the surgery, the doctor declared, "We got it all, but you really need to have radiation and chemo." Once again, JJ declined, but wondered what she might further do to help facilitate her healing.

It was the morning of Easter Sunday, one of JJ's favorite holidays. "I sat down and conversed with my Maker," says JJ. "I asked, 'when I go to church today, can you show me a sign of what I'm supposed to do?'"

As the crowd began to pour into the church, she took a seat, and a woman whom she did not know sat down next to her. A few minutes later, the woman reached into her purse and pulled out two objects, one of which she handed to the person on her left, and the other of which she handed to JJ on her right. Each had been given a small Easter egg-shaped rock with a word on it. JJ's rock was a beautiful shade of pale green. She couldn't help but notice that the purple writing on her rock perfectly matched her dress. The inscription? It simply read: "Miracle."

"When I saw that sign, I knew I was going to be okay," says JJ. Every three months, she went back to be examined, and a year later, received a letter from her doctor which read, "Congratulations! You are cancer-free."

JJ continued to work on her attitude. She also started going to an ashram and began to incorporate yoga and Qi Gong into her schedule, along with 45 minutes of walking every day.

One day, she met a man at the ashram who appeared to be in great pain. "I think you need a miracle," said JJ, as she put the rock in his hand. The man, who looked like he might be dying, began to steadily improve.

Months later, when he looked well, JJ asked if she might have the rock back, but the man was not yet willing to part with it. A few years later, however, when he felt more secure about his health, he returned the rock to JJ. What day was it? Easter Sunday.

The rock began to find its way into the hands of others, who also experienced major turnarounds in their health. Pretty soon, a friend of JJ's said, "You need to dispense more miracle rocks to people." So JJ began collecting rocks from all kinds of sacred sites. Says JJ, who now sports a smile on her face more often than not, "I guess you could call me an 'M.D.' – I'm a 'Miracle Dispenser.'"

Miracle Thinking Tips

- Do certain rocks, or rocks with specific inscriptions, hold miracle powers or give off healing energy? Some people might think so, while others may not. Is it the belief system of the holder of the rock that accounts for major turnarounds in health? Some people might think so, while others may not. Is it the hope or increased faith that someone feels when given such a rock that contributes to her healing? Some people might think so, while others may not. Is it the doctor who performs the surgery that accounts for the healing? Some people might think so, while others may not. Is the idea that rocks heal people something that only someone from California might believe? Some people might think so, while others may not. Are all these possibilities true? What do you believe?

✦ When you face a scary unknown, set strong, clear boundaries as to what you are willing or not willing to accept as part of your experience. While JJ faced many unknowns, she set strong, clear boundaries as to what she was willing to accept – a lumpectomy, and more invasive surgery; as well as to what she was not willing to accept – radiation and chemotherapy. By setting strong, clear boundaries, you will be more empowered to deal with challenging situations.

✦ Be willing to look at your possible contribution to a problem. JJ asked herself, "What have I done to attract this experience?" It was only when she was able to obtain the awareness that "life is too hard. I don't want to be here," that she was able to make a conscious decision to choose life.

"Whether it be money, a relationship, or anything else – in order to attract something different, you must become someone different."

– Elyse Hope Killoran

For Striving to Become More of Who You Are . . .

Initiation

Prosperity Coach, Elyse Hope Killoran shared the following story . . .

A piece of clay sat in the potter's studio. Everyday, it watched as the potter picked up another piece of clay and transformed it into a beautiful vase. Feeling jealous, the clay shouted, "Pick me! I want to be a vase, too!"

One day, the potter picked up the piece of clay. Excitedly, the clay exclaimed, "Today, I will be a vase!"

The potter proceeded to pound the clay on a tray. Then he cut the clay into strips and kneaded it. The clay said, "What are you doing? This is abuse! Put me back on the shelf!"

But the potter just kept on going and began to spin the clay on a wheel until it was totally dizzy. Finally, the potter stopped. Breathing a sigh of relief, the clay declared, "Thank God, it's over."

But no sooner had the words been formed when the potter put the clay in the kiln and boiled it alive. When the potter removed the clay from the oven, the clay ranted and raved, "How dare you?!"

Next, the potter covered the clay with a glaze that made the clay feel uncomfortable and tight. Then he put the clay back in the kiln to be baked again. The clay despaired, "I won't make it another step."

Finally, the clay was removed from the kiln and placed on a shelf, where it began to pray, "Please leave me alone and never come back. I don't want any more abuse." But a little while later, the potter came back anyway.

"Stay away from me! Don't you dare touch me!" said the clay. "I can't believe what you've put me through!"

The potter replied, "Do you want to see yourself?"

The clay said, "Leave me alone. I don't want to go anywhere with you!"

Very gently, the potter said, "Look," then held the clay up to a mirror. The clay saw that it was now a beautiful vase. The potter said, "This is exactly what you asked for. You asked to be transformed into a vase. You just wanted to wake up one day and be a vase, but that's not the way it works. This is what it takes, clay. You have to go through all those steps."

Miracle Thinking Tips

- "Whether it be money, a relationship, a new home or anything else – in order to attract something different, you must become someone different," says Elyse. "In some way, you will have to change. Just like the clay, every desire you have is, in reality, the beginning level of an initiation, and you will have to walk through your road of trials to get to the other side."

* "Realize that every block you encounter is part of your hero's journey," she continues. "The block is an opportunity given to you by the universe as your key. If you can embrace the block, integrate it, and dissolve it away until it's no longer an issue, you will be stronger, more powerful and more focused. At that point different opportunities are free to come to you."

* "When you declare yourself to be something, everything that is the opposite of what you've just declared will usually come streaming into your life. Recognize that this condition is only temporary. If you welcome the process, you will move fluidly to the other side. But then, you'll only stay on the other side for a short while because there will always be the next mountain that you'll want to reach, and in order to get there, you'll need to be someone different once again."

"To receive a message from a departed loved one, you must be available. If you are wailing with grief, you will not be able to receive the message."

– Barbara Brennan

For Evidence of Life After Death . . .

A Promise Kept

Dallas Franklin was in a computer class when she heard the news – her dear friend, Tom, probably wouldn't make it through the night. Since the hospital was next door to the college, luckily, she didn't have far to go. With tear-laden eyes, Tom's family greeted her warmly at the entrance to the hospital room.

Tom had been struggling for the past seven months. Knowing that he might not be here much longer, just last week, they had spent the afternoon together, listening to music videos and talking about old times. Dallas had also asked Tom if he'd send her some kind of message when he crossed over to let her know that he was still around and doing well. Although he had laughed at her request, he agreed to do what he could if he found himself still 'living' after he 'died'.

Then the fateful day finally arrived. Tom knew it was his last night. He was in a great deal of pain and the massive medication he had been given was causing him to hallucinate from time to time. At one point, he told his family he wanted to go outside for a smoke before he went to sleep that night.

How does one go to sleep, knowing they will probably not wake up in this world? The question raced through Dallas' mind as she attempted to come to terms with his leaving. Before their visit ended, she hugged him lightly; his body was in too much pain to squeeze harder. As his family returned to the room, she choked back her tears, then went out into the hallway where she let them spill over. Tom passed away that night.

A few months later, Dallas decided to adopt two kittens from a local farm. The mischievous duo brought her much comfort and joy. Each day, the playful pair would meet her at the door when she came home from work. One day, however, they were nowhere to be found. She looked under beds, tables, behind dressers, etc. No cats. No one else had a key to her apartment and it appeared that nothing had been tampered with. So, where could they be?

As she double-checked every room for a second time, she began to replay the time before she had left for work. Perhaps they'd snuck into the clothes closet while she had been getting dressed. She opened the closet door – no cats.

The only place she hadn't checked was a small sunroom, which had always been kept closed, since it was only used for storage. Besides, it was so hard to open the sunroom door, what was the point? However, with no other option available, she pulled hard on the door. Much to her surprise, two very yappy kittens came running out.

Dallas was stumped. How could the kittens have possibly gotten in there? She didn't have a clue.

A short time thereafter, a new psychic arrived in town. Dallas decided to go for a reading. Near the end of the session, she asked the psychic if there were any messages from Tom. The psychic picked up a tablet and began to draw. She drew a picture of the sunroom door, complete with its tiny window and little curtain. Dallas didn't say a word, but waited patiently. When the psychic finished, she said, "Tom wants you to know he put the kittens in the room. Do you understand this?" Then she continued, "He also wanted to tell you he really likes the cat, 'Boots.'"

Dallas was flabbergasted. She hadn't named the cat with the four white paws, the one that was now being called, 'Boots', however, she had mentioned to another friend a couple of weeks prior that if a child owned him, he'd probably be called, 'Boots.'

Dallas received her message and Tom kept his promise.

(*This story first appeared on Dallas Franklin's web site, www. giftsofdivinity.com, and is used with permission.*)

Miracle Thinking Tips

* Says Dallas, "If you make a contract with someone before they pass, that promise is always sacred and is kept. Tom found a way for me to believe that he was still alive and doing well. He made his promise and got his message back to me. It was never 'good-bye' when I last saw him, but rather, 'so long, until we meet again.'"

* According to after-death researchers, Bill and Judy Guggenheim, authors of *Hello From Heaven*, there are numerous ways to receive communication:

You can hear a voice; feel a touch; smell a familiar fragrance; sense them around you; see them in a dream; notice the sudden appearance of natural phenomena, such as a butterfly or a rainbow; see a partial or full vision of the person in a suit of light or as they appeared on the physical plane; witness changes in electrical objects, such as lights flickering or a TV or radio turning on and off; notice mechanical objects being activated for no apparent reason; or find other objects in places where you know you didn't put them. Your loved one may also contact another person to deliver a message to you. (www.after-death.com).

❧ Barbara Brennan, author of *Light Emerging*, states that not only does a departed loved one have a 'gift' that they want to give you, but that it hurts them if they can't get through to you because your grief is so overbearing. If you can find a place of quiet and peace inside of yourself – even in the midst of your grief – you may be able to receive the message, or 'gift,' that your loved one has for you.

"You have the ability to imbue inanimate objects with energy that can make you or others feel better."

– Ellen Henson

For Understanding Our Connection to All Things . . .

The Adventures of White Bear

With certain trepidation, White Bear hesitated as he was carried aboard the plane. All he knew was that he was on his way to some place in the world called, 'Australia.' Once there, Rita, the volunteer courier for a stuffed animal project called, "Animal Beacons of Light," would travel far across the land until she found a hospital or orphanage where he would be given as a companion to somebody he didn't yet know.

At first, White Bear found himself squished into an overhead bin, but a short while later, a flight attendant asked if he might come out and visit with the other passengers. White Bear was relieved. After all, it wasn't easy for a three-foot-long bear with short arms, long dangling legs, and feet that jutted out, to fold himself into such a tiny space.

White Bear happily made his way from person to person. One of these people was a little girl who was about six-years-old. Like White Bear, she, too, was afraid; her family was emigrating to a new country and she had no idea as to what to expect. For a long time, she and White Bear chatted about their respective fates.

A stewardess overhearing the little girl's conversation relayed the following to Rita: "When the little girl said goodbye to White Bear, she said, 'Good luck White Bear. I hope you find a good home. At least I know where I'm going, but you don't even know where you are going.'"

As she left the plane, the little girl looked happy; she was clearly no longer distressed about her new adventure in life.

Rita never shared the story about White Bear with anyone on the plane. How did the little girl know?

Miracle Thinking Tips

- ✦ You have the ability to imbue inanimate objects with energy that can make you or others feel better. Says Ellen Henson, founder of Animal Beacons of Light, "We take stuffed animals and fill them energetically with love, well-wishes, prayers, and comfort. Then we send them out to children of all ages who live in dire circumstances as a reminder that someone somewhere cares about them."

- ✦ Take a class with someone who can show you how to work with energy. Ellen, who is a Reiki Master, explains that she fill the animals with Reiki energy, which is "a form of energy that is about compassion, balance and centering." Then she "attunes the stuffed animals to carry the energy so that wherever they go, the Reiki energy will flow. The bear can then connect to the energy itself and draw it in and pass it on," she says. "You might ask, 'how can an inanimate object do that?' Just look at a watercolor painting. It's an inanimate object, yet it can make you feel differently than how you felt a second ago. In the same way, the little girl understood the plight of the bear because she picked up on the energy."

✦ "There is a piece of Spirit in everything." The way to see it? "Find that Divine aspect of it. Connect with your own Spirit first, then state: 'Everyone I meet and every place I go, I find the spirit of that person, place or circumstance.' Keep your heart open and see the highest good in any situation."

"In Spanish, 'mira' means 'to see.' A miracle means to see something differently. Anything can become a miracle if we want to see it differently."

– Sandy Alemian

For Coping with Loss...

Getting the Message

Pacing the floor of the Neo-Natal Intensive Care Unit on a daily basis was the last place Sandy Alemian ever expected to find herself. However, when her second daughter, Talia, was born but refused to nurse, the infant had been hurriedly transferred to the NICU unit for testing. Ten days later, the doctors delivered the news no parent ever wants to hear: If Talia even made it through the newborn period – which was highly unlikely – she would never be able to talk, walk, eat, breathe on her own, or communicate because of the severity of abnormalities in her brain.

Although Sandy had two miscarriages prior to conceiving Talia, her pregnancy had been normal with no complications during the birth. A very positive person, Sandy refused to believe the harshness of this news. In fact, she knew in her mind that Talia was going to be her 'miracle baby'; if she just prayed hard enough and sent Talia enough positive energy, she knew she could make her well, and prove everybody wrong.

At three weeks old, the doctors advised that the fragile infant would probably live no longer than 24 hours once she was taken off of life support. However, when the respirator was removed, Talia started breathing on her own. "See? I knew it! I knew she was going to be okay!" thought Sandy, who had visions of being on Oprah with her 'miracle baby' as she inspired other mothers onward to victory.

Still, clearly, Talia was not out of the woods, and besides flopping on her bed and crying a million tears every night, Sandy decided she'd better prepare herself in other ways, just in case. "What kept me going was crying on my bed," she says. "My prayers turned from, 'God, you *have* to make her better,' to 'God, whatever I need to deal with, just give me the strength.' This change in prayers constituted a huge shift in my experience. This prayer kept me going and gave me a sense of peace. I felt a connection to an all-powerful, all-loving presence that I know is always with me whenever I choose to feel connected to it."

Journaling was another way in which she took comfort. "Writing has always been a way for me to connect to God and my angels and the wisdom of my soul," she says. Immediately, Sandy began receiving messages as she wrote. "These messages were more powerful than any drug I could have ever asked for. I would ask for guidance. I wrote directly to God asking, "How do I get through this?"

Whether the messages were coming from her soul, God, or her angels didn't matter to Sandy. "The thoughts were coming so fast and furiously, my pen was having a hard time keeping up," she says. The messages, which talked about death from the soul's perspective, explained that there was much more going on than what we could see. Sandy was comforted by the messages, which "were very reassuring, calming and loving. I was gently guided by a source who knew that I would be okay," she says.

Talia died at 31 days old. Within two weeks, Sandy, who was in a state of despair over her tragic loss, hoped that she would die, too. "You can't get away from your own pain," she says. It's everywhere you are, no matter where you go. I just wanted to get out of my skin."

When her sister suggested that she might find relief in journaling, Sandy went to find a pen. She says, "As I sat down to write, in my inner ear I heard, 'Mommy.' I thought, 'Nope. I'm not going there.' Then I heard, 'Mommy. Mommy. Mommy.'" This time, Sandy allowed herself to write what she heard.

"I believe this message was from Talia's spirit," she says. Talia told Sandy that she could feel the love from everybody in the hospital even though she couldn't show it back.

A few years later, Sandy felt a presence around the back of her head one day, as though somebody was trying to get her attention. When she turned, of course, there was nobody there. Later that day, she brought her older daughter, and her son, who had been born a year and a day after Talia's death, to a playground. As the children ran off, once again, she started feeling this presence around the back of her head. Again, it felt like someone was trying to get her attention. Just then, two women came over and sat down on the next bench. Within a minute, one of them turned backwards, and looking toward a group of trees, yelled out, "Talia! Get out of the woods, honey. You're going to get poison ivy." A little girl quickly came running out of the woods.

"That was Talia giving me a sign: 'I came, Mommy. I'm here,'" says Sandy. Eventually, Sandy's journal grew into a book called, *Congratulations, It's An Angel,* in which she documented and shared her experiences and communications with Talia.

"Talia was an earth angel who came to me to help me change my life. Going through the experience of loss gave me my mission in life – to help others through their dark times, because once you've been through the darkness and you are on the other side of it, you can go back and reach out your hand to someone else."

Miracle Thinking Tips

* Says Sandy, "When you go through a loss, you can easily feel like all hope is gone. How do you then start over again? Well, remember the Weebles who wobbled but wouldn't fall down? We can be like the Weebles if we want to be. When we fall down, there's some part of us deep down in our hearts that is going to get us back up again . . . always, always, always. It's there for us if we want it and are willing to choose it."

* "Your angels are available to give you advice about every big or little thing," she continues. "If you want to communicate with God, or your angels, guides, or loved ones in spirit, invite them to help you." Then sit quietly and ask a question of them. Begin to write your answer without censoring the information that is flowing to you. "Doubts, such as, 'Is this message coming from me, or is this coming from them?' 'How can I be sure?' or 'How do I

know it's not just me?' can come in. What is of vital importance is to trust the information you receive." The more you do it, the more your confidence will build.

✳ Inner gifts to our soul often result from the experience of a major loss. As a result of Talia's death, Sandy became a different person with a new set of priorities and a new mission in life. She further believes that "our experiences in life are not meant to victimize us or hurt us, but rather, are to help us grow and evolve and deepen our relationship with the Source. In Spanish, 'mira' means 'to see.' A miracle means to see something differently," she says. "Anything can become a miracle if we want to see it differently."

"Choices in your highest and best interest make you feel enlivened. Choices that are not may make you feel tired."

– Kathleen Casey

For Instructions on the Path . . .

The Peacemaker

Kathleen Casey always wanted to be a peacemaker. In the early '80's, she devised a plan to help achieve world peace by connecting business people with one another throughout the major financial centers in the world. After all, would you go to war with people you personally knew and with whom you had financial connections?

At a time when networking was an almost unknown concept, she first initiated her idea by hosting networking events where businesspeople could meet one another in Northern California. However, just at the point when her events became wildly successful and she was about to obtain international sponsorship through a major hotel chain, the whole kit and kaboodle collapsed.

What do you do when your great idea, your dream, seemingly goes down the drain? Having no clue as to what life held for her next, shortly, Kathleen was introduced to a man who presented conflict resolution workshops worldwide. During the course of the workshop, Kathleen met yet another fellow, Jim, who offered advanced conflict resolution training to corporations. Impressed with his abilities, she felt a spontaneous desire to work in conjunction with Jim, but had no idea as to how that might happen since she was a novice and he was a well-seasoned professional.

As fate would have it, though, by the end of the workshop, she was able to experience her first taste of being a mediator when members of the center where she was staying were experiencing a conflict. Using her innate abilities, Kathleen helped them find a way of bringing their conflict to a mutually satisfying conclusion.

Surprisingly, when she arrived back home in the Bay Area, a message asking her to mediate awaited her on her answering machine. The person who had left the message had no idea about her interest in mediation; he just trusted her and that is why he had called.

A number of small opportunities trickled her way, but Kathleen was still barely able to support herself. Was being a mediator her true calling? She decided that the best thing she could do would be to take some sort of action, and if this was really the right path, something would have to happen. She decided to contact one of the large hotels, and to her delight, wound up being offered a position that hadn't even existed before – training employees in a newly designed customer service program. Eventually, she found herself mediating a variety of conflicts as the hotel went through serious financial difficulties, ending in bankruptcy. When the hotel finally folded, Kathleen expected her job to go with it. Instead, the company that took over hired and trained her to train their managers in leadership for six months.

At the end of the time, however, there she was, once again left without any visible means of support. Sitting in meditation each morning, she would ask, "What do I do now? What steps should I take?" Every day, she received the same reply: "Do nothing." This was hard advice for the go-getter who was willing to take action to make magic happen in her life.

One day the phone rang. Remember Jim? Two years had passed since their last conversation. Now a large corporation wanted to hire Jim for a 3-year program, which would involve conflict resolution, communication training and team building. Since 98 percent of the organization was made up of women, they wanted him to work in conjunction with a female co-leader. Was she interested?

Although she wasn't yet a certified mediator, Kathleen jumped at the chance to be interviewed. She was nervous about her resume, though, which would never compete with the likes of more experienced corporate trainers. As it turned out, no one ever even looked at her resume. The man who hired her simply told her he was looking for people with heart; and for that, she clearly was qualified.

Kathleen then began to more fully live what she considers to be her soul purpose. Although this purpose was revealed to her in a different form than she had initially imagined and intended, this new form turned out to be both financially beneficial and more soul expanding in ways in which her intellect could not have known or planned.

Miracle Thinking Tips

- "Are you ready to jump into your dream? Then create from your heart, rather than from your intellect," says Kathleen. "When you create from your heart, your personality is in alignment with your soul. I had a spontaneous desire in my heart to be a peacemaker. My heart said, 'Oh yes! This feels right.'"

- To get clear on your desire, "your body will give you more information than your intellect," says Kathleen. "State: 'I am going to (<u>fill in the blank</u>),' or ask yourself, 'Do I (<u>fill in the blank</u>)?' Observe your body's reaction. Does your breathing become shallow or more expansive? When you take a huge breath, your body is saying, 'yes.' Choices in your highest and best interest make you feel enlivened. Choices that are not in your highest and best interest may make you feel tired."

- "Through movement or by making sighing sounds or toning, you can release old patterns and emotions that do not serve you so that you can more easily feel what your body is telling you. Close your eyes and sense if there is a place in your body where you are drawn. As you focus on that sport, allow the body to express whatever it wants to express through breathing, sighing, moaning, or other sounds or movement. Do not scream or rage. That would be a form of forcing. Let the sound come from a very relaxed and gentle throat, and allow the body to do what it needs to do without interference from the intellect."

"We live in a neutral field of energy. We sculpt it with our words and beliefs. Throughout the day, this neutral energy is waiting for our command."

– Peggy Black

For Believing in the Mystical . . .

The Heart of Mu

When an ultrasound revealed that Peggy Black's daughter would not be able to have a child due to the presence of scar tissue in her uterus, Peggy offered to help. Having her daughter relax on a massage table, Peggy, who uses sacred sounds for healing, placed her hands on her daughter's abdomen and chanted tones into her belly. While Peggy toned over her daughter, they sensed a 'presence' in the room. At one point, her daughter reported that it even felt like her mother's hands were inside her body, providing both comfort and healing.

By the end of the week, after her daughter had flown back to Hawaii where she lived, Peggy received miracle news: "Mom, I think you'd better sit down. They ran another ultrasound and there's no scar tissue. The doctors did a second procedure and adjusted my hormones and now my uterus is clear and healthy." Peggy and her daughter were ecstatic.

A few months later, there was a second miracle to report:

"Mom, I'd like you to go outside and look at the most beautiful thing you can find." Peggy went out into her garden and looked at the huge array of blooming flowers that were growing there. Then her daughter said, "I want you to know that I'm pregnant."

Before the due date arrived, Peggy knew she just had to find a way to get to Hawaii for the grand occasion. And as long as she was going to be there, perhaps she could share the use of sacred sounds with others and even do some private sessions. Besides teaching others about their healing benefits, this would also give her the opportunity to raise the $1000 she needed to cover her expenses back home while she stayed in Hawaii.

Before she flew to Hawaii, and with her daughter's help, she arranged to give a free talk at a local hospital on the island. Peggy felt quite positive she would attract private paying clients as a result. She also happened to listen to a local radio show, which featured a psychic. When she called the show and told the woman about her upcoming plans in Hawaii, the psychic replied, "You have done sacred sound work there before. It was in the heart of Mu." Although Peggy had no idea what the "heart of Mu" was, the message felt encouraging.

Trusting that she would somehow raise the $1000 she needed, Peggy flew to Hawaii to see her new granddaughter who had just been born. A few days later, her talk at the hospital appeared to be well-received by the thirty people who attended, but not one person booked a session.

With tears rolling down her cheeks, Peggy prayed: "God, you know that I am here to serve. You know that I am here to share sacred sounds with others and you know my needs. I am grateful for Your support in any way that you can offer it."

Serenity immediately replaced her anxiety. "I was in a place of gratitude, knowing that everything was in Divine Order," says Peggy. "Then, when I looked up, I saw a gorgeous rainbow outside the window."

The next morning, the phone rang. A woman who ran a local radio program had heard about Peggy's talk and wanted her to come to the station for an interview. The radio interview went well, and afterwards, she invited Peggy, and her daughter and new granddaughter, Emily Sarah, to join her and seven of her women friends for lunch.

As they arrived at the home of the woman hosting the luncheon, the door opened and the host said, "Welcome to the heart of Mu."

"I still didn't know what the heart of Mu was, but I got covered with chills," says Peggy.

Inside the home was a huge geodesic dome, which was referred to as 'the meditation chamber.' After lunch, the women went to the meditation chamber, where Peggy led them in a 'Welcoming Ritual' to honor the birth of little Emily Sarah. Much of the ritual included the toning of sacred sounds. By the end of their sacred time together, two of the women had requested private appointments with Peggy.

Says Peggy, "When I did the session for the first woman, I scanned her body energetically and sensed a blockage in her abdomen. She shared that she had always had problems with this area. Then I had a vision: I saw myself in the Temple of Dendara in ancient Egypt, which was an ancient sound healing temple. In my vision, I saw this woman had come to me as a neophyte of thirteen years old, to be trained in sound healing. She had gone out into the surrounding community where she had been sexually abused. Someone had carried her back to the temple, where she lay bleeding, and I couldn't stop it. She died."

With tears rolling down her face, Peggy described the scene to the woman, then said, "Allow me to heal what I was not able to heal at that time."

When the session ended, the woman expressed her gratitude, laid some money down on the table, and walked out to her car. Peggy accompanied her out. When she went back inside, Peggy discovered the woman had left $600. Racing back outdoors, she tried to convince the woman that she had paid way too much. The woman replied, "First of all, it's probably not enough for what you just did, and second of all, that is what I was told you needed when I was in meditation this morning."

By the time Peggy returned to the mainland, her prayers had been answered: she had $1000 in her purse.

Miracle Thinking Tips

★ Says Peggy, "We are either in miracle thinking or victim thinking; the universe will honor either one. We're the ones who decide what it's going to be. Since I live my life believing that everything is a miracle, the universe outdoes itself to bring me outrageous and wonderful miracles." Living her life from this particular framework, Peggy acknowledges that miracles occur in every aspect of her life.

★ "We live in a neutral field of energy," Peggy explains. "We impact it, and affect it, and sculpt it, and arrange it with our thoughts, words and beliefs. Therefore, with every action throughout the day, I am aware that this neutral energy is waiting for my command. For example, if I am getting ready to go somewhere, the first thing I do when I get in my car is to sculpt the experience I want to have. I'll say, 'I am grateful and I allow Spirit to clear the way, to provide Divine protection and to guide me in a safe and smooth and timely arrival at my destination.' Every time I do this, the traffic parts and leaves my way clear."

If you receive something from the universe that you asked for, but it wasn't exactly what you wanted, "thank the Universe for what it did provide for you, then ask for the thing that you want and be clear. If something doesn't come forth, like the job you want, say to the universe, 'If the most perfect job for me is not available at this time, please give me a "bridge job" to bridge the space, or provide me with financial support, until mine appears.' If you are patient enough, the universe will provide it."

"Talk about whatever it is that you want to create and keep those thoughts in the back of your mind. To create something, start by focusing on something small."

– Mike Fink

For Fulfilling a Desire . . .

The Meeting

Mike Fink was devastated when his 79 year old father went off and married a 23 year old, who clearly wanted his money. Shortly afterwards, when his father told him that he no longer wanted Mike in his life, the young investment banker, who lived in Paris, found it impossible to shake the depression that hung over his head. Every day, he trudged off to work, where he would put in at least sixteen hours before he trudged home.

One day, he happened to pick up a book by a French fashion designer named, Paco Rabanne. Although people in the United States might not recognize that name, in France, he would be considered in league with designers like Ralph Lauren.

The book spoke to Mike in that it contained a lot of the designer's esoteric beliefs, which were in line with his own way of thinking. Mike was struck by the fact that this man, who was very successful in the outer world, was willing to risk his reputation by writing about a subject that many would consider with suspicion or find unacceptable.

After reading all three of Paco Rabanne's books, Mike felt like he had to meet this inspirational messenger. However, what were the odds that this meeting might actually take place?

Says Mike, "Imagine reading a book by Ralph Lauren, then deciding you would like to meet him. You might live in New York where he also lives, but cities like Paris and New York are huge. How could it ever happen?"

Mike playfully pondered how he might meet the author. For starters, he began asking everyone he met, "Do you know Paco Rabanne? I've been reading his books and I'd like to meet him." Unfortunately, his queries only led to dead ends. Mike was not to be deterred, however. He constantly imagined their meeting in his mind. With a childlike innocence, he even thought to himself, "When I meet him, what shall I call him? 'Paco?' 'Mr. Rabanne'?"

Although Mike usually worked until midnight, one evening he finished at 7 p.m. Normally he would have hailed a cab, however, since it was such a beautiful evening, he decided to be a little more out and about in the world and take the bus. But the bus he needed, which was on the opposite side of the street, was beginning to take off. Waving his arms like a madman, he rushed across the oncoming traffic and persuaded the driver to open the door.

As the bus rumbled toward an intersection many stops later, Mike noticed a man crossing the street in front of him. It was Paco Rabanne. Since there was no bus stop at that particular corner, Mike had to plead with the driver to let him off, insisting that he absolutely had to speak with the man walking across the street. The driver finally opened the door and Mike sprung across the intersection in search of the man, who was now waiting for his own bus.

Excitedly, Mike walked up to Paco, introduced himself, and said, "You know, Mr. Rabanne, this meeting is no coincidence. I have called this meeting."

The two proceeded to engage in a lively conversation, and when Paco's bus came, he let it go by. At the end of their talk, Paco said, "Mike, it was very nice meeting you and I wish you a wonderful journey," (meaning the journey of life), "but I think that our meeting is a coincidence. You didn't call this meeting."

"Mr. Rabanne," Mike responded, "you've been living in this area for a long time and I've been living here for fourteen years, and yet, we've never had a chance to meet before today." Mike thanked Paco for his time and left.

"This was a small miracle," says Mike. "It was such a dark period in my life. I was depressed and I couldn't see any way out. Meeting Paco Rabanne uplifted me. It wasn't so much what he told me as it was the experience of meeting him. This encounter made me feel like a guardian angel was telling me that there is hope after all. It made me feel like there was a light at the end of the tunnel."

Soon afterwards, Mike quit his job to go into management consulting, and finally decided to follow his heart and got a Masters in psychology. Although he was never able to reconcile his relationship with his father, he no longer works until midnight anymore, and now has a radically different career that makes his heart sing.

Miracle Thinking Tips

- ✦ "Talking to others about things that you desire as if they've already happened, or with a certainty that they will happen energizes those things," says Mike. "Talk about whatever it is that you want to create and keep entertaining those thoughts in the back of your mind. In my mind, when I had thoughts about what to call Paco, I was posing these questions with the certainty that this meeting would take place. In my mind it was going to happen or it had already happened."

- ✦ "When you start talking to others about what you want, you can often manifest your desire much faster. Others might offer new possibilities, ideas, or solutions to potential obstacles that you might not have considered."

- ✦ "If you want to create something, start by focusing on something small." For example, "If you were going to a gym, you wouldn't start out by benching 300 pounds. You'd start much smaller. Focusing on something small will get your manifesting muscles going so you can create whatever it is you want in your life."

"Align yourself with outrageous joy. Then things will flow more smoothly, people and resources will appear as if by magic, and miracles will occur."

– Suzanne Baker

For Impending Surgery . . .

The Party Hat

When Suzanne Baker heard the news that she had cancer in her bottom eyelid, at first, she felt tremendous apprehension then disbelief. The news that her doctor would not be able to perform surgery to determine the extent of the cancer for at least three more months left her feeling even more upset. However, as a Miracle Thinker, Suzanne decided that staying in fear and being upset would not help her situation. Instead, she chose to focus on the outcome she wanted, which was to have the surgery within the week, before her new teaching job started. A few days later, the doctor's office called. They could fit her into surgery that week.

Still feeling fearful a few days before the surgery, Suzanne realized she would need to reframe the whole situation if she wanted to create a better outcome. She decided to think of the upcoming surgery as a party in which she would be the guest of honor. The doctor's office called on three different occasions to change the time for the surgery. Each time, Suzanne expressed her excitement about the plans they were making for her party. The night before the surgery, she also had a chakra-balancing energy session with a woman who could help her relax and prepare even more for her party.

On the morning of the surgery, instead of feeling fearful, Suzanne awakened in peace. When the doctor's office called to confirm that she was on her way, she told them, "I wouldn't miss my party!"

Arriving at the surgical unit, she wore a 'party hat,' a straw voters' hat with a red, white and blue ribbon around it, which was significant for her because her birthday was on July 4th. Red, white and blue were colors that she always wore for her party on her birthday.

"This is my party hat," she told everybody. "Let's go to the party." Of course, all of the surgeons and medical personnel appearing in their scrubs were all wearing their own 'party hats.'

Although Suzanne didn't know one person in the town in which the surgery was taking place, the R.N. who prepped her for the operation turned out to be a close friend of a friend of Suzanne's who lived about 45 minutes away. Their connection felt serendipitous, and when the RN asked if she wanted a tranquilizer, feeling completely at ease, she declined.

Suzanne's party attitude began to spread outward. A young man, who was being prepped for surgery behind an adjoining curtain had overheard Suzanne's party talk. As he was being wheeled to his surgery, he said, "Let the party begin!"

Next, the anesthesiologist arrived. His 'party hat' featured an assortment of red, yellow, orange, pink, and green canines against a blue background. Suzanne and the doctor began to banter as though they were old friends sharing a laugh. Continuously, she felt no fear about what was about to happen, even though the doctor warned her about the stinging that might occur as the anesthesia was administered, or the nausea she might experience afterwards.

When she was in the surgery room, the medical team made a big production over her hat, which by this time had acquired a baby blue, surgical hair net that was perched on top of its midsection. The straw brim stuck out around the perimeters.

Befuddled, one said, "What is this here for?" Another replied, "That's her party hat." The anesthesiologist said, "Let her keep it if it makes her happy." Laughing, a nurse replied, "Well, this is a first." Their laughter lightened up the energy in the surgical room.

The surgery was entirely successful. The cancer had been isolated in a very tiny area. Suzanne felt no stinging from the anesthesia and no nausea afterwards. She remained happy to have had such a fun party. During what most people would consider to be a very stressful experience, it seems that the more she reached for joy, the more it kept unfolding.

Miracle Thinking Tips

- ☀ Says Suzanne, "When you align yourself with outrageous joy, everything lines up. Outrageous joy puts you in alignment with God, and the Universe, and your Higher Self. Then things flow more smoothly, needed people and resources appear as if by magic, and miracles occur."

- During Suzanne's party, she became aware of a rhythm, which she describes as a "Divine Motion" that is always going on beneath the surface of our lives. "There is an Eternal current that flows through all of the circumstances of our lives, regardless of our ability to perceive it or not. To tap into this current, you've got to get to that place where the things of this world do not interfere with your ability to feel at peace." Suzanne transformed a state of fear into not even needing a tranquilizer. By taking herself to a party, she was able to tap into that Eternal current of well-being where all she could perceive was peace and joy. And as she tapped into that current, the synchronicities and miracles lined up for her one after another.

- Whining, moaning, complaining, and negativity don't win points on a Miracle Thinker's scorecard. Do whatever it takes to calm your "monkey mind" where your thoughts and fears ramble on in your brain. Let go of the victim stance, and step into a place of empowerment in the midst of difficult situations. Every time you find a way to lighten up, even if only a little, good things will begin to happen.

Author's Conclusion

What I've learned from the many "Miracle Thinkers" I've interviewed, and as mentioned in the Introduction, is that each of us holds a piece of the Miracle Thinking puzzle. There are many different attitudes, thoughts, and beliefs that can contribute to the creation of miracles. However, if I had to condense them, I'd say that some of the top Miracle Thinking principles are as follows:

1) The Universe likes a good target.

In order for a miracle to occur, we must ask very clearly for what it is we want.

2) The Universe will never give you a 'yes . . . but.'

This is one of the most important, and often trickiest, of principles to understand. Many of us are quite good at declaring our target, whether it be a new job, a healthy relationship, 'x' number of dollars, healing the world in some way, etc., however, we often unknowingly cancel our intention in the same breath. For example, we might say or think, "I want a relationship," then we'll mumble to ourselves, "but I don't want to get my heart skewered again like I did in that last relationship." Or, "I want a new job . . . but I never want to work for someone like that boss ever again."

A 'but' that is voiced at a conscious level, or hidden in the subconscious, will keep the energy flow of a miracle from coming your way.

If you are claiming that you want something to occur in your life, look for any 'buts' that might be lurking under the surface.

3) *The Universe has a bigger plan for you than you have for yourself.*

Accepting an award on a televised awards show, Oprah once said, "I always believed that God had a bigger dream for me than I could dream for myself, so I always ask, 'What is Your dream for me, and will you allow me to live in that dream'?' If you want to create a multitude of miracles in your life, allowing yourself to live in 'God's bigger dream' for you will help to open new doors that you couldn't even possibly imagine might open for you.

4) *It's not about knowing the right answer; it's about asking the right question.*

This is a quote from transformational facilitator, Gary Douglas (www.accessraz.com). You don't need to know everything about how to accomplish your goals. Just ask open-ended questions, such as the very powerful question Oprah asked above. Then allow the Universe to fill in the blanks of your life for you. It always will.

5) *The Universe can only give you as much as you are able to receive.*

Many people are comfortable in the role of giver, but feel entirely uncomfortable when it comes to receiving. If you say 'no,' or feel any sense of resistance when you are offered a gift of any kind, you have set Principle #2 into motion: *The Universe will never give you a 'yes . . . but.'* The more you say, 'no' to the little gifts that come your way, the more you close down the opportunity for bigger gifts to reach you. On the other hand, if you keep saying 'yes' to the little gifts that are offered and put up no resistance, your 'yes' will continue to take you further and further in the most positive direction.

6) *Reach for joy.*

Every time we lighten up, good things happen. Keep reaching for joy as much as you can. Make up reasons to feel joyful in situations where you normally might feel triggered. For example, laugh or sing in your car while driving in rush hour traffic. Or find something to compliment about the person behind you when you are in a long checkout line at a supermarket and the person at the front of the line is purchasing an item with no price tag on it and a clerk is now wandering the store looking for its cost. Engage in joyous conversations rather than in negativity. You will immediately step into a place of empowerment. Then watch for miraculous outcomes.

7) *Just do it!*

Miracle Thinkers take action. They don't just sit around waiting for miracles to happen. When you are clear on which way to go . . . step forward. Every time you come up with a great reason as to why you didn't accomplish what you said you intended to accomplish, say to yourself, "the dog ate my homework." It's all just an excuse. You will see that what is stopping you is some sense of underlying resistance. Since the Universe will never give you a 'yes . . . but,' if you find yourself saying "the dog ate my homework" frequently, you'll know you've chosen a direction that is not in alignment with your core at this time, at which point, you can choose again.

We've got this little space, called, 'life'. . . and it happens between birth and death. It's just this little space with our name on it, for however long we have it, so please make the best of it. Apply some of these Miracle Thinking tips and come up with more of your own. The more you develop your Miracle Thinking mindset, the more miracles will flow to you.

Want to strengthen your Miracle Thinking mindset? You can become part of the Miracle Thinking community at www. MiracleThinking.com.

Author

Randy Peyser is the author of *The Power of Miracle Thinking; Crappy to Happy: Small Steps to Big Happiness NOW!; What Sign Are You in DOG?; The Write-a-Book Program; The Mind, Body, Spirit Speakers Guide;* and *The Internet Marketing and Publicity Directory.*  Randy owns Author One Stop, a national publishing consulting firm that helps people write and publish books. Services include: book editing, book proposals, ghostwriting, book publicity, help finding agents and publishers, and self-publishing. For author services, please see www.AuthorOne Stop.com. For information on Miracle Thinking seminars, or to schedule a Miracle Thinking talk or workshop in your area, please visit www.MiracleThinking.com.

Contributors

All of the stories in The Power of Miracle Thinking are true. If you are inspired by a particular story, you are invited to contact the person who lived that story and tell them how they have impacted you.

Cari Alter has a spiritual counseling and healing practice in Northern California where she helps people connect more deeply with themselves in order to bring peace into their lives. She offers sessions in person and by phone worldwide, and is the author of *Breaking the Myths of Reality*. www.carialter.com

Terri Amos is a spiritual coach, wife, mom, the author of *Message Sent: Retrieving the Gift of Love,* and its companion meditation CD, a former "Miss USA" and television host, and now the host of internet radio's, *The Family Connection,* on www.HealthyLife. net, www.terriamos.com.

Suzanne Baker is the creator of Personal Mind Training. She holds teaching credentials from the State of Texas and the State of California. A Certified Firewalk Instructor and an NLP Practitioner, she specializes in helping men and women remove the obstacles that stand between their dreams and the life they really want. She has fourteen years of public speaking experience and is the author of "Step into Your Power: 25 Ways to Change Your Life!" www.randypeyser.com/stepintoyourbeauty.com.

Krystyna Barron teaches empowerment workshops for women. She is a facilitator of Access Energy for Transformation. With loving energy and laser-like precision, she helps individuals get to the core of their issues, release them, and gently guides them to a new level of beingness, so that joy and ease can flow more naturally into their lives. accessjoy@hotmail.com.

Peggy Black is a "Sacred Sound Salutarist" who founded the International Sound Symposium. She is the creator of the "Morning Messages," now received by thousands of people around the world, and author of *The Chantnal*. She uses her voice and psychic abilities to assist clients and groups in creating miracles through workshops and private sessions. www.peggyblack.com, www.morningmessages.com.

Kathleen Casey is a transformation and wellness facilitator who utilizes all her skills and experience to assist clients to integrate the effects of their sessions into real change in themselves and in their lives. Kathleen travels, giving workshops and private sessions in person and by phone. E-mail brochures are available. kcasey@cybermesa.com.

JJ Crow is the creator of "The IAM Cards," which help individuals to discover their most fulfilling possibilities. Through her cards and private sessions, and as a mentor, speaker, workshop leader and yoga teacher, JJ helps individuals find the answers they are seeking to create more joy in their lives. www.joymentor.com.

Mike Fink works with people who want to dramatically increase their income. He is a Master Practitioner in Neuro-Linguistic Programming, a Certified NLP Trainer, and a former investment banker. He assists people in achieving a wealthy and fulfilling life by helping them to change their core limiting beliefs. www.magician within.com and www.wealthymindworkshop.com

Dallas Franklin is a Canadian fated by her name to live in Texas. She lives with her husband, Eric, whom she met on the Internet, and their beloved Kipper Kat. Dallas helps writers at http://sell-writingonline.com, and offers divine angel and psychic consultations at http://giftsofdivinity.com.

David Franklin is a professional teacher, counselor, guitarist, and author. He regularly teaches personal growth workshops, performs classical and improvisational guitar, and is the author of the *Note-A-Day Calendar Series*, which features music lessons for different instruments for every day of the year. www.DavidFranklin.org, www.EvolvingCulture.com, and www.InstrumentCalendars.com.

Elissa Rigzin Giles received gifts of insight and healing from the "Unified Field." In 1997, she experienced a wave of shakti (energy) so strong that it gifted her with enlightenment and the ability to channel shakti to recipients to help them clear blocks to their authentic self and establish their own magnificence. shaktiwise@comcast.net.

Lila Davis-Harding believes the ability to clarify your intention is the single most powerful ability one may possess. She offers coaching on how to gain clarity and declare your intentions in such a way that you experience receiving what you want in your life. www.changemyworld.net.

Ellen Henson is accomplished at traveling to "other worlds" and bringing information back to this one. Practicing Reiki, producing essences and teaching aligned energy practices are ways she assists clients in transforming their lives. She is a Reiki Master, essence producer, A.L.I. teacher, hand analyst, planetary healer, and founder of Animal Beacons of Light. www.animalbeacons.org.

Reverend Christine Hodil is a clairvoyant healer, counselor, channel, initiator, mystical educator, improvisational vocalist, voice teacher, percussionist, and dancer. An ordained minister in the Order of Melchizedek, she offers in-person and phone sessions, and can be sponsored in your area for group or individual work. www.sourcehealing.org.

Elyse Hope Killoran is the President of "Prosperity from the Inside-Out" and the creator of the online "Prosperity Game." Find the game, along with free resources to help you "play your way to prosperity," at www.ChoosingProsperity.com/free.htm.

Mary Ellen is known as "Angel Scribe" to thousands of internet newsletter readers, and fans of her best selling books, *Expect Miracles* and *A Christmas Filled with Miracles*. She believes, and teaches, that we can all become a vehicle for miracles to work through us to touch the lives of others. For her free email newsletter: www.AngelScribe.com.

Debra LeForest is recognized as a leading edge, sound therapy pioneer. The inventor of a Day Spa Sound Therapy Treatment, she is a musician, recording artist, and radio host. She is also one of the first to have worked in a medical facility as a Vibroacoustic Practitioner and Sound Healing Researcher. Soundconnexions@yahoo.com.

Rayna Lumbard, LMFT, CPC is a Marriage and Family Therapist, Certified Professional Coach, Hypnotherapist, and Transformational Intuitive Healer. She inspires individuals, couples, and families who are challenged physically, mentally, emotionally, and spiritually. Rayna is also the founder of The Awareness Network, a networking and educational organization in San Jose, CA. www.InnerSuccess.com.

Dawna Markova is the founder of SmartWired, which offers educators around the world a new way of teaching children. Rather than label children as learning disabled, ADHD, or any other labels, her approach is to teach educators how to become aware of each child's unique learning style and use their individualized learning styles to develop their natural gifts and talents. www.smartwired.org.

Norman Mosher, computer whiz and consultant, has traveled the entire US, much of Canada, and loves to play in the Old World. A white water river guide, he also has experienced underwater archaeology in Jamaica and has worked on a cruise ship to Alaska. Working in the field of sustainable energy is his current passion. Normanmosher@aol.com.

Nadia McCaffrey is the founder of "Angelstaff" and "Changing the Face of Life." Since the death of her son, Sergeant Patrick Ryan McCaffrey, a National Guardsman in Iraq, she has been working to end the war, to help American soldiers, and to provide help for Iraqi children and their mothers. www.angelstaff.org, www.patrickspirit.org.

Thomas Oates is the creator of the award winning video, *Pacific Light*, and other high quality video and audio products in which he incorporates healing music and imagery to move people in the direction of the healing peace of God's presence in the present moment. www.healing-peace.com.

Barb Rees inspires writers on their way to publishing success. She leads writers' workshops and retreats, and is the co-founder of an annual Festival of Writers. A dynamite speaker, she is the author *of Lessons From the Potholes of Life*. To move your dreams forward, contact "Dreambuilder Barb." Dreams Inspirations Seminars, http://dreambg1.blogspot.com, http://dancewithlife. blogspot.com.

Rev. Katherine Q. Revoir, creative mentor, spiritual counselor, speaker, and doodle instructor, is the author of *Spiritual Doodles & Mental Leapfrogs, a Playbook for Unleashing Spiritual Self-Expression* (Red Wheel/Weiser), *and CREATE! A Sketchbook and Journal* (Chronicle Books). As a teacher and student of Truth, she writes humorous workshop and class curriculum. www.SpiritualDoodles.com.

Kathleen Ronald guides individuals and businesses to create incredible transformations in record time. Dubbed "the mind chiropractor," she combines Neuro-Linguistic Programming with Divine Inspiration to take the kinks out of one's thinking and help her clients shift from sabotage to success. www.speaktacular.com.

Betty Sayers, author, grant writer, poet, and beekeeper returned to her hometown, Holdrege, Nebraska, where she and her sister, Nancy Herhahn, invented an economic development enterprise, Business Beyond the Farm. Betty writes stories about entrepreneurs in southwest and south central Nebraska who have a vision and act to benefit their community, as well as themselves. www.businessbeyondthefarm.com.

Suzka! is the creator of the "No Handshake Pin" (© 2001), which she designed after multiple surgeries made it difficult for her to shake hands with people. Her hope is that the pin will become a universal symbol for recognizing those with similar conditions. She resides in Portland, Oregon. www.suzka.com.

Una Versailles is a pseudonym for this Twelve-Step author, who wishes to remain anonymous out of respect for the tradition of Twelve-Step programs. Una is a spiritual counselor and a published poet.

Steven Walters is a singer/songwriter who performs nationally at New Thought churches, spiritual retreats, workshops and conferences. His CDs, which evoke the peace that happens when we allow ourselves to Be, include: *"Just This Moment"* and *"So Many Blessings."* His music is performed by Tom Rush on "Wildflower," a Judy Collins compilation. www.stevenwaltersmusic.com.

Karen Williams is a humor columnist and the author of *Soulsongs: Manifesting Your Deepest Desires,* a collection of inspirational writings that explore the importance of mental focus and the role of emotions as a guidance system. Karen lives in Orlando, Florida, with her daughter, Emily, and Hamlet-the-Hamster. To receive her newsletter: www.karenwilliams.net.

9540547R0018